7010490 9

NO DADDY! NO!

As Told by Olivia Clark

Written by Rob Winkworth

ARCHWAY
PUBLISHING

Copyright © 2016 Olivia Clark.

All rights reserved. No part of this book may be used or reproduced by any means,
graphic, electronic, or mechanical, including photocopying, recording, taping or by
any information storage retrieval system without the written permission of the author
except in the case of brief quotations embodied in critical articles and reviews.

Archway Publishing books may be ordered through booksellers or by contacting:

Archway Publishing
1663 Liberty Drive
Bloomington, IN 47403
www.archwaypublishing.com
1 (888) 242-5904

Because of the dynamic nature of the Internet, any web addresses or links contained in
this book may have changed since publication and may no longer be valid. The views
expressed in this work are solely those of the author and do not necessarily reflect the
views of the publisher, and the publisher hereby disclaims any responsibility for them.

Any people depicted in stock imagery provided by Thinkstock are models,
and such images are being used for illustrative purposes only.
Certain stock imagery © Thinkstock.

ISBN: 978-1-4808-3660-0 (sc)
ISBN: 978-1-4808-3661-7 (e)

Library of Congress Control Number: 2016915193

Print information available on the last page.

Archway Publishing rev. date: 10/11/2016

We exist as women who are Black, who are feminists, each stranded for the moment, working independently because there is not yet an environment in this society remotely congenial to our struggle – because, being on the bottom, we would have to do what no one else has done: we would have to fight the world.

Michelle Wallace - From <u>A Black Feminists Search for Sisterhood</u>

If Black women were free, it would mean that everyone else would have to be free since our freedom would necessitate the destruction of all the systems of oppression.

The Combahee River Collective

For too long a time
the heat of my heavy hands
has been smoldering.

Cherrie L. Moraga – From <u>The Welder</u>

CONTENTS

1

On a cold, fall day, Olivia's house sits on a tired suburban street. The houses are mostly well kept, but a few stand out. All have the familiar look of row houses. There is little life on the street despite the fact that it is the middle of the day. Olivia's house sits across from a small park with worn play equipment. The park is attached to an abandoned school. It looks like no one has been there in years. Some windows are boarded.

A nice, white Jeep Cherokee, Jennifer's car, pulls up in front of Olivia's house. The engine is still running and Jennifer and Dexter are still inside the car. Jennifer's look of trepidation at Olivia's house shows that she has never been in this sort of neighborhood in the city. She looks a little nervous as she grips the steering wheel tighter and tighter. Then there's Dexter, sitting in the passenger seat, unfazed by anything.

Jennifer goes on to say, "This is it?"

"Yes Jennifer, that's Olivia's house. Let's go," Dexter says as he opens the door to get out the Jeep.

"Dexter? Is this…are we?..."

"This isn't Afghanistan, Jennifer. Come on; we're fine. Don't be a silly, sheltered white girl."

As Jennifer turns off the car, she looks at Dexter with a sharp stare, "But I am a silly sheltered white girl. I can't help it."

They both exit the car and Jennifer moves to the back of the Jeep to open the hatch. When she realizes she is all alone, she looks up in a panic and sees Dexter walking to the house. "DEXTER!" She screams a little louder than intended.

Dexter frustrated, responds, "What?"

"Could you come help me?"

Dexter unwillingly walks back to the Jeep and looks inside the open hatch. Inside lies a fancy computer case, Jennifer's Burberry backpack, and other fashion accessories. She hands Dexter the unexpectedly heavy backpack and it weighs a ton.

"Jennifer, What the hell you got in here?"

"Nothing. Just things we might need."

"Heaviest 'nothing' I've ever lifted," Dexter replies as he throws the backpack on his back. As Jennifer grabs the rest of her stuff and closes the back trunk, she pushes the fob on her keys four times. Once to lock it, secondly to hear the horn, again to lock it, then finally to hear the horn once more for assurance.

With a smirk, Dexter looks back at Jennifer, "Jennifer, I think you got it."

They walk up to the door of Olivia's house and Dexter pushes the ringer. The front door is protected with a locked swinging gate that is painted white. This fact is not lost on Jennifer as she stares at the gate and nearby surroundings, hoping Olivia is not home.

From behind the door, Olivia asks with a hard voice, "Who is it?"

"It's Dexter, Mrs. Clark. Toby's friend?"

A latch is disengaged and Olivia opens the door. It's dark inside. Jennifer and Dexter can hardly see her behind the gate. Olivia regards the visitors and then unlocks the gate and lets them in. Dexter walks into the house, but Jennifer looms outside.

As Olivia gets a better look at Dexter, she smiles. "Yes, Dexter. Come in now. I'm so glad you're here," she remarks as she gives Dexter a genuine hug. "Let me look at you. It's been a little while. In college now, right? It's treating you well, I can tell that. And who is your friend?"

"This is Jennifer, my friend from school. The one that I told you about."

"Come in, Jennifer. It's all right; I won't bite." Olivia laughs and she motions for Jennifer to come in.

When Jennifer walks in, she and Dexter see Olivia clearly for the first time. She is a friendly woman with a warm and knowing smile that belies her seventy-six years. She holds a cane in one hand, and although bent with old age, she stands strong and welcoming.

"Hello, Mrs. Clark," Jennifer says with a fake smile and uncomfortable look on her face.

"It's my pleasure, and please, call me Olivia. You too, Dexter! I think you are old enough now that we can pass on ceremony, especially since Toby is not around. Come in, you two. Let's find a place where we can talk."

Olivia takes them into the dining room where a high wooden table sits right in front of a large picture window that looks out on the street where they can see Jennifer's Jeep and the vacant school yard. The room is cozy and dark. Jennifer is busy organizing her bags, and Dexter sits across from her. Olivia finds a seat at the head of the table.

As Olivia gets comfortable and crosses her feet, she looks over to Jennifer. "Now Jennifer, tell me. Why do you want to talk to me?"

Jennifer, surprised, looks at Dexter, and Dexter returns Jenny's concerned gaze as if to say, "I told her".

"I thought... Did Dexter tell you?"

"Oh he told me, but I want to hear it from you. That's all."

Jennifer looks around the room trying to get comfortable again. "Ahh... I am working on my graduate thesis. It's about the challenges of women in Detroit, specifically the struggles women faced around the time of World War II and the riots. And Dexter said that you had...well...a..."

"A 'colorful life' might be a nice way to describe it."

"Well…yeah…from the little that Dexter told me, it sounds horrific."

Olivia looks at Jennifer with a seriousness. "It was at times. I will tell you everything and I think, after it all, you will have one amazing story to tell. But first, I want you to understand, that as awful as everything might sound, I thank God for the challenges he brought me because they gave me my family. And so while you might think it all sounds…horrific, do me a favor, and remember through all this, my life has been blessed."

Jennifer looks at Olivia and pauses. Olivia's intensity takes her back a moment. "Okay…"

Olivia then goes on to tell her story. "Okay. Now, let me see. I was born in 1938 in Mississippi. My mother grew up there, but my Daddy was from Alabama. He came to Mississippi as part of the CCC and he was working there when they met."

"The CCC was a work program from the depression era…right?" Jennifer asks as she pulls out her laptop.

"Yes, it was called the Civilian Conservation Corps and he worked there, in West Point Mississippi, when he met my mother. The men were working on establishing the…what was it now…the Tombigbee National Forest and my momma and her family were living in West Point, just a little bit north of there."

2

It is the morning outside of the workers camp in West Point, Mississippi. An open flatbed truck travels through the small city center of West Point. A young woman, known as Tiny, walks along the side of the road with her sister while carrying an infant, Diane. The man in the passenger seat of the truck, Eddie, watches Tiny as him and the driver ride by.

The truck slows down at the general store in the heart of the town. The driver and Eddie exit the truck and enter the GENERAL STORE OF WEST POINT. It's a typical general store with a large counter that is organized and filled with a variety of goods. A worn out shopkeeper stands at the register. "What is it today, boys?"

The driver replies, "We just need us a few bags of that bone meal. Ran into some tired old soil down the forest way."

"You have the order form?"

The driver hands over the order form to the shopkeeper. Eddie hangs back and wanders absent-mindedly around the store as the negotiation goes on. With the ring of the door-bell, Tiny, her sister, and Diane enter. Simply dressed in worn, red blouses with faded blue jeans, and penny loafers, the sisters are focused on their conversation as they walk in. Both women are looking at fabric. Eddie watches them as he walks over.

No one hears the exchange, but whatever Eddie is saying is engaging and makes both women laugh. Tiny hands Diane to her sister and turns to Eddie.

The driver, having received the order back from the shopkeeper, looks around for his friend. When he sees Eddie and the sisters talking, he is not surprised at all. "Eddie! Come on. We ready here."

Eddie turns and looks at Tiny, "I'll see you tonight?"

Tiny stands still at first, and then shyly nods. Eddie with a happy grin, returns her nod and says, "Tonight then."

After running to the driver, Eddie grabs a large sack of bone meal from the floor. He picks it up like it's nothing before turning back to Tiny and giving her one more smile. She smiles back and carries on with looking at fabric.

The boys leave the general store, load their bags in the back of the truck, and get in.

The driver then turns to Eddie. "You gonna hit on every woman down here?"

"Can't help it. So many beautiful women."

"Well, you better leave something for the rest of us."

Eddie grinning, "Not if I can help it."

3

It's a hot summer night, and there's a shack bar right outside of the worker's camp. It sits like an oasis in the darkness just off the main road. A few yellow lights and candles flicker throughout the ramshackle bar. Eight or ten tired and dirty men from the CCC camp are loosely gathered around over-turned crates. Behind a makeshift bar of torn up wood, an old bartender stands. He's ready to serve his patrons from a makeshift shelf behind him that holds only a few bottles of unmarked whiskey and other liquors. A large tub of ice and water sits to the side, filled with cold beer.

With a beer in front of him, Eddie sits at a wood crate at a wooden table, facing the entry to the Shack Bar, and talking with the driver. There are 2 empty chairs at the table. Eddie stands out. Clean and nicely dressed, his attitude and polish stands out from the group. The men are talking, laughing, and enjoying the respite from a hard day's work. Music plays from an old record player. It's the tunes of Motown.

Tiny and her sister, walking, emerge from out of the darkness. They wear simple dresses, different from earlier in the day. Tiny is wearing a green dress that shows her cleavage well, hugs her waist firmly, and fans out from her waist to the bottom of her knees. Her sister is wearing a form-fitting red dress that pushes up her breast and stops right above her knees. Eddie immediately spots the young women, and escorts them over to his table. He helps the young ladies sit down and offers to get them something to drink. He brings back a cold beer for each and sets them down as he sits next to Tiny. Again, no one hears them talk, but it is clear that Eddie understands how to make her happy. In no time, they are all laughing and enjoying their time together, but Eddie slowly isolates himself and Tiny. The evening moves on with both of them getting closer and closer.

Eddie catches a song from the record player and picks up Tiny to dance with him. He escorts her to a tired patch of dirt amongst the tables. They start dancing easy and slow, but slowly, the beer and Eddie's hands bring the two into a close sensual dance. The music gets louder as they grow closer and more sensual. Eddie's hands easily lasso Tiny, and she submits to his touching and manipulation. The music pulses, then slowly fades as the lights around them die and their interaction moves into complete darkness.

Moving to a private dark place, they find solace by the trees, away from the noise of the Shack Bar. Eddie pulls Tiny's dress up as he presses against her. They begin to have sex, and Eddie moves with an intoxicated energy of his own while Tiny enjoys the ride as well. Their moans of pleasure die with time amongst the deep dark forest, and they are left with darkness.

The following day, Eddie goes to Tombi National Forest where he works amongst a group clearing the trees. It is 10 am in the daytime and the workers are sitting and standing by their bunks. They are quiet and pensive listening to the CCC Director.

"Gentlemen, you all have made some great contributions here at the National Forest, but it is time for most of us to move on. Most of the men stationed here will be moving on to other camps to work on different projects. Jensen and Hildabrush here will pass out the new assignments. If you are moving on, transportation will be tomorrow morning at 9:00am. Thank you gentlemen. That is all."

Jensen, a wiry man in a well-groomed uniform, walks down the aisle passing out letters and waiting by the beds. Eddie sits on his bunk near the front of the room, waiting for his letter. Jensen hands it to him and waits. Eddie checks and sees his name, opens it and regards the letter, but he can't tell what it says.

Eddie hands the letter back to Jensen, "What's all this mean, Jensen?"

"It means they are transferring you up to Shuqualak to work on building the new Air Force Base."

"Shuqualak?... Where the hell is that?"

"It's down south... Little more than 50 miles south of here."

Eddie with a concerned tone, "I can't leave here. I just got me a wife."

"Well, things will be just like they've been Eddie. We'll just send your pay to your new family."

By the look on Eddie's face, a spark is lit. "The hell you will."

Jensen, puzzled at Eddie's reaction, fires back. "Actually, you are right. We sure as hell will. That is what you signed up for – it's what I have to do just as much as anyone here with a family. The money goes to your families until your time here is done. That is what we will do. If you have a problem with that, you will have to take it to the director. But he ain't gonna be able to do nothing for you."

Jensen hands Eddie back the letter. He takes the letter and watches as Jensen moves on to the next bunk, waits, and reads the letter for the man.

Eddie says to himself as he folds up the letter and packs up his gear, "I gotta get out of here."

Eddie then goes back to Tiny's house that night and talks to her about the plans his job has for him. Tiny is not thrilled but she loves Eddie and agrees to go along with it. The following morning, Eddie is transported in a bus with other CCC workers to Camp Anders.

***

Back in Olivia's dining room, she continues to share her story with Dexter and Jennifer. "Daddy moved from camp to camp. My momma stayed with her family in West Point. I was their first child born in

1938 when Daddy was off working. My momma and her sisters pretty much raised me and my sister Diane, and then my brother Jake."

Jennifer so intrigued by Olivia's story, asks, "Who was Diane?"

"Diane was my mother's daughter. She was from another father, though momma never told us who he was…"

"So she was older than you?"

"Yes. Diane was 3 years older than me. She was always beautiful… from my first memories of her, she was lovely as a flower.

Olivia quiets for a moment as Jennifer makes a few notes. "So, after your dad finished up in the CCC, that's when you came to the city?"

Olivia smiles as she reminisces. "Yes, that's correct. I was maybe four or five at the time. I don't really remember. But all kinds of folks from the south were getting work up here at the auto plants. My daddy got a job at Fred's Auto, making cars, and we all moved into the projects at Hammond and 6 mile."

4

1940s – Detroit. It's Saturday and Eddie's house is a new, single family home. His block is filled with row housing, but has nice yards and crisp streets. Cars pass on Hammond, children run down the street, and the city is alive. Eddie and Tiny's house is painted red with a yellow, front door. The colors are vibrant and distinct compared to the rest of the homes on the street. Olivia, seven, and Diane, ten, play in the front yard.

Eddie pulls up in his Cadillac, and the girls frantically step away to give him space. In one swift motion, Eddie pulls far into the driveway. He steps out, dressed in a fancy, custom, and tailored brown suit with a yellow shirt. He wears a brown hat. As he emerges from behind the car, he looks up to the window of his next door neighbor, Ms. Lewis, and flashes a smile. Olivia and Diane lean to look down the driveway. Eddie, caught eyeing Ms. Lewis, turns on the kids. His eyes take on "the look" – the girls run to the far side of the front lawn before he even says something. He follows them to the front of the house. Olivia and Diane go back to playing together – they look nervous now, hoping Eddie does not come to them. Eddie stands behind them, eyeing Diane…contemplating. He takes off his suit coat and hat, holds them in his hands, then moves to the front door, opens it, and walks in.

Eddie looking for his wife, "Woman?"

Tiny, pregnant with Eddie Jr., comes out of the house and takes the red wagon that was nestled by the front door to put the groceries in. They didn't have much money. Well… Eddie did, but he wouldn't share it much. He would give Tiny $20 every Saturday for the week's groceries, and that was it. Eddie appears from the front door, shirt now off, wearing suspenders over his tank top and smoking a cigarette. "Woman… You take Olivia with ya now."

Olivia and Diane are holding hands and a nervous look overcomes both their faces. Tiny gives Olivia a look. "Come on now, Olivia."

Olivia withdraws from Diane after holding hands as long as possible. Diane stands still. Olivia and Tiny walk down the sidewalk to the grocery store. Olivia looks back over her shoulder at Diane remaining still.

Eddie calls Diane inside. "Hey girl…come on inside now."

Diane reluctantly turns to the house and walks up the steps. Olivia turns back and sees Diane walk through the door as Eddie closes the door behind her.

Later that day, Olivia and her mom return home from shopping. There is an anxiousness about Olivia. As the house gets closer, Olivia leaves her mom and runs into the house. Diane is sitting on the couch. She is still and looks as if she has been crying. Olivia goes to sit next to her and regards her as she takes her hand. "You okay, Diane?"

Diane nods.

"Did something happen?"

Diane just shakes her head.

Tiny from outside the house, "Olivia! Eddie! You get yourself out here and help me with these groceries!"

"Come on Diane, let's go help momma." Olivia stands up and takes Diane's hand. She stands up slowly, somewhat painfully, and then joins Olivia.

Olivia and Diane load the groceries and help Tiny as Eddie comes from upstairs and sits down in the living room.

***

Back in Olivia's living room, she continues with her story. "Every Saturday, momma would go to the grocery store with twenty dollars, and make it last the week."

Jennifer shocked, "How could he do that? You had four people in the family and Eddie Jr. on the way."

"Even when there were ten or eleven of us in the house, it was always the same...twenty dollars."

Dexter amazed, "So how did you all make it?"

"Daddy never bought us new clothing or shoes. We wore hand me downs often too small or large. We didn't complain because we thought that was the way it was supposed to be. It wasn't that he couldn't afford it. He just didn't care. No one knows when exactly Daddy changed into an evil person. It seemed like it happened over time as I had more brothers and sisters on the way and that meant less and less money for him. I don't think he looked at Momma the same either. Her body changed over the years from having children and doing a lot of home, labor work and he just seemed unattractive to her because his eyes always wondered to younger women. He didn't even love us that much because we ate food out of garbage cans, pieces of old bread, and candy with rocks in it. But we didn't care; we just picked out the rocks and ate it.

"We didn't get breakfast or lunch. The school didn't provide anything. We just had to make do with what we could. You'd be surprised what people would throw out – perfectly good bread, or a piece of chicken that was only half eaten. I would pick through the garbage and all the neighborhood kids would be walking by as they went to school. They looked disgusted at what they saw and laughed at us."

Jennifer with a look of despair, "That sounds awful."

"It might have been, if we weren't starving. I would wait for kids to throw out their lunch, grab their bags, and find a half-eaten sandwich, a discarded apple, take it, and go to sit at a lunch table with some girls that were my age. They would look at me, then get up and leave.

"But we got used to it… you learn to appreciate what you are given… and see how wasteful people can be. I'd even find a piece of gum that somebody had spit out, and once you cleaned it off, it would taste pretty good." Olivia laughs. "It really would."

Olivia, still laughing, stops. "You'd be amazed what you could learn to live with."

Jennifer starts scribbling some notes. "What do you mean?"

"Diane," Dexter says after realizing what Olivia meant.

Olivia nods.

Jennifer sympathetically questions, "Diane…was being abused by your father? By Eddie?

"I don't know how she learned to live with it."

5

The girls are asleep in their shared twin bed. The room is dark, but the lights of the city come through the single, open window. The room is small, hardly enough room for a small bed and space to walk around it. A tired blue blanket covers the bed. The girls are restful.

The door slowly opens and Eddie walks in, carrying a flashlight. Olivia is sleeping towards the door and the light shines right into her eyes. Eddie holds it there, regarding Olivia, seeing if she is going to wake up. She doesn't and stays the same as when he walked in. Eddie moves around the side of the bed, places his hand underneath the blanket and moves his hand up Diane's leg, uncomfortably too high, and points the flashlight in her face. "Girl, get up. I need you now."

Diane replies still half sleep, "Daddy… please no. I'm so tired."

Eddie takes the flashlight and hits her in the face. Forceful, but not overly powerful. "Now, you get up."

Diane, clearly in pain, but understanding, moves to get up. She steps in front of Eddie and walks out of the room, Eddie following her. He looks back at Olivia, still sound asleep, and closes the door. Olivia's eyes pop right open. She lays there, the pressure of the world is suddenly felt in those eyes, hoping nothing happens. But it always does.

Diane walks down the hallway. It's dark, and foreboding, and she walks slowly. The slightest whimper can be heard. She enters the bathroom, and Eddie reaches over and turns on the light. "You take off that night shirt now, girl."

Eddie closes the bathroom door. Olivia's eyes widen as she listens to the muffled sounds of Eddie talking to Diane. Moments of quiet, then the sounds of Eddie building up and achieving orgasm. The sounds pound on Olivia. Her eyes stay wide open; a cold, sad stare fixed on the doorway. Silence. There are steps down the hallway. Olivia closes her eyes. Diane enters the room and quietly gets back in bed as she places a quarter on her bedside table. Olivia opens her eyes and stares at the door as Diane cries next to her. Eddie was giving her money along with threats of killing her if she told momma.

6

Diane, Olivia, Jake, Eddie Jr., and Donald the infant, are all around the living room area. Tiny is pregnant with Paul. The four oldest kids are dressed for Church and Tiny and Eddie are still wearing their night clothes.

Sundays are always special days. On Sundays, Eddie makes the kids pancakes, and the house feels light and happy. See, Sundays are church days, and that means the worries that the kids carried all week would disappear.

When it came to Sunday school, the kids always walked. Eddie never dropped them off. But when Sunday school was over, they couldn't walk home fast enough. They would change out of their Sunday clothes, carefully hang them up, and then run to the living room. The kids, Diane, Olivia, Jake, and Eddie Jr., would all loosely line up, waiting for Eddie, who would eventually emerge from the bedroom and hand each child a quarter to go to the movies. The kids had to be back by 4, no matter what. Most times, they only had about 15 minutes to see a movie.

They would always run to the theater with smiles on their faces. It was the only time they could just be themselves. It was the mid-1940s, all the kids wanted to be themselves.

They would run in after buying their tickets, slow down by the concessions just for a beat, and look at the popcorn and candy that folks were buying wishing it were theirs. Eddie never gave them money to buy snacks, or allowance money. He treated them as if they were a burden to him. There was no love on his part. It was this same Sunday afternoon when things played out differently, however. Eddie Jr., Jake, and Olivia started to move pass the concession when Diane started walking back. Olivia looked back at Diane with questioning eyes. "Diane… where you going?"

"I'm gonna go get some popcorn."

"How are you gonna get popcorn?"

"I have some money," Diane responds as she pulls all the quarters from her purse.

Olivia's mouth drops. She comes over to Diane and talks in an amazed whisper. "How did you get some money?"

"Daddy."

"Daddy gave you money?"

Diane nods and moves on to the concession stand. Olivia steps back to take it all in. Maybe somewhat realizing what was going on, Olivia moves up to Diane to help her.

Olivia and Diane look through the glass case with wonder. "What should we get?" Diane asks her sister as she smiles in excitement.

"Popcorn?"

"What else?"

Olivia dumb-founded by Diane's response moves in closer to Diane. "What else? How much money you got Diane?"

"Fifty cents."

Olivia's eyes widen. "Well, then, we should get some candy too."

Diane hands over the money to the lady at the concession and then hurries to the screening room. She and Olivia walk in burdened by popcorn, candy, and a soda pop. They have surrounded themselves with the spoils.

When Olivia notices it is too dark to find her brother, she whispers a shout into the darkness, "Jake!"

Jake sticks his head up and the girls spot him. They go over to him and sit down in the row. Jake is wide-eyed as the girls pass down some candy and situate themselves. "How did you get all this?"

"Diane got it."

Diane interrupting Olivia, "I found it."

Olivia looks at Diane, again pondering and a little slack jawed. Diane looks at Olivia. "Right outside the theater. I found it."

The kids sit back, diving into the snacks. They eat like they are starving. Jake, excited that they finally get to eat popcorn and watch a movie, "This is gonna be the best movie ever."

The room darkens even more and the movie, *Abbot and Contello Meet Frankenstein*, plays on the screen. The kids are all into the movie, except Olivia is not with them. She snuck off to go to the bathroom. They continue watching the movie when Olivia runs up. "It's 3:40. We gotta go!"

Jake upset, "But the movie isn't done."

Diane frustrated that Jake wants to act like a baby, "Jake, we gotta go! Come on Eddie, let's go."

Eddie Jr. gets up with Diane and starts to leave, but Jake stays put. "I'm staying. Gonna watch the end of this part."

Olivia upset, "Jake, we gotta go. We can't be late."

"I'll go. Just a few minutes."

Diane looks to Olivia, "I'll take Eddie. You watch a few more minutes then run home. You should be alright. Bet you'll beat us home."

Olivia agreeing with her sister. "Okay."

Olivia sits down as Diane and Eddie Jr. walk out of the theater. They watch the movie, a scene where Costello is walking quietly down the hall and Frankenstein suddenly starts chasing them. Costello finds Bud Abbot and speaks in gibberish about what he saw. Jake genuinely laughs, "So funny."

Olivia knows it's nearing four o'clock, "Okay Jake, we got to go."

Jake whiney but understanding, "Okay..."

Olivia and Jake run from the movie theater. They run fast. As they get close to a busy intersection everything suddenly stops. A car accident at the intersection has collected tons of cars. It's gruesome. Two cars are ripped open in the intersection, bodies are noticeable, and the kids are taken back by the horror for a moment. It's clear that people were killed. The crowd of onlookers grow as police quarter off the area of the intersection, extending almost for an entire city block. Walking out of the trance of the accident, the kids frantically try to cross the intersection, but are pushed by crowd and police farther from their destination. They eventually find a hole at the far end of the block and run.

Olivia and Jake run up the front steps of their home. They run in the door, panting, hard out of breath. Diane and Eddie Jr. sit on the couch. The house is quiet. Tiny is still at the church helping the other women prepare for Tuesday's bible study. Olivia and Eddie Jr. look at Diane, who looks away.

Eddie emerges from the bedroom and he is wearing his t-shirt and pants. His eyes are wild and something is sticking out of his pants pocket. The kids see it coming. He looks at his watch. "You're late."

Olivia panicking, "Daddy, there was an accident... We would have been..."

Before Olivia could finish her sentence, Eddie slaps her in the face. "Don't talk to me girl."

Eddie grabs Olivia and pulls her to him. He takes her, face down, and traps her head between his legs. From the pressure he exerts on her neck and head, the tears start to roll down Olivia's face.

Olivia bawls, "Daddy! Please... No!"

Eddie, squeezing his legs tighter, yells, "I said don't talk to me, girl."

Eddie takes an old section of a garden hose, with the connector on the loose end, out of his pocket. It's a thick old-fashioned heavy hose. He lifts up her dress to expose her backside. He beats her...

hard. She squirms in pain. Eddie closes his legs tighter. Jake looks on in fear… crying.

Eddie closes his legs together even tighter. "Stop your moving, girl."

Eddie continues beating Olivia, then releases his legs and lets her drop. She lays on the floor. He then goes to Jake and repeats the beating. Jake takes it and cries. The beating is not as bad. Jake is younger and Eddie seems to tire out. Eddie releases him, lets him drop to the ground, and walks out. Diane and Eddie Jr. are sitting on the couch, scared and trying not to look at their brother and sister lying on the floor.

7

Olivia's family is preparing to go to the store. Diane, Olivia, Jake, and Eddie Jr…

Olivia's family is preparing to go to the store. Diane, Olivia, Jake, and Eddie Jr. are all gathered around Tiny. The kids and Tiny, plainly dressed in simple hand me downs, are sitting…waiting. This is a moment of possible joy, especially on the nice spring day it appears to be. Yet, they are waiting for Eddie to bring them their weekly grocery allowance, and to tell who can go on the shopping trip.

Eddie enters the room. More fanciful than the others, he dons nice slacks with suspenders over a t-shirt, exhibiting a style that is his own. The family quiets as he enters the room, and he is carrying his Bible.

Eddie reaches into his pocket and pulls out his wallet. He gives Tiny a twenty dollar bill. She reaches for it and he gives it reluctantly. All the kids are waiting. Eddie with disgust, "Take Diane."

The other kids pause. There is relief for Diane, which Olivia also feels for a moment, but then disappointment and then a little concern arises. Staying home with dad is not something for which the kids wish. Tiny looks displeased, but then moves with Diane to leave. Olivia steps forward as if to go. Some fear begins to kindle. Tiny looking at her says, "Stay with daddy, Olivia… We'll be back soon. Why don't you play with your doll?"

Olivia dutifully obeys her mother and goes to her doll to play. The Caucasian doll, peaking from beneath the couch, is tired, ratty, and looks unloved. There is a quiet to the air as Tiny and Diane leave and the rest of the family retreats to their own space. Eddie watches them leave, looks over at Olivia, and then moves to the bedroom. Olivia remains in the living room. She is quiet, but wary, and continues to play with the doll.

Eddie with a calm and sweet voice says, "Girl! Come here. I have something I want to tell you."

Olivia, taken back and a little scared responds, "What is it daddy?"

"It's a secret, sweetie…"

Olivia gets up with the doll in her hand. She thinks for a minute. She decides to drop it on the ground and walks to the bedroom. The room is dark and heavy. Eddie is sitting on the edge of the bed with his Bible between his hands. He is looking at Olivia as she stands in the doorway. He takes the Bible and slides it under the bed where he is sitting. "Come here, girl."

Olivia doesn't come right away.

"I got a little secret we can share. And if you keep our secret just right, I'll get you that nice little Easter dress I keep hearing you talk about."

Olivia steps in, but still keeps her space.

"There ya go…this gonna be just between us. Won't that be fun? To share a secret?"

Olivia, concerned, "Can I tell mommy?"

"No. Wouldn't be much of a secret then. This is a secret just between you and me."

There is a pause. Olivia's discomfort is palpable. Eddie leans in, "You ready?"

Olivia just nods.

"Good. I need you to take off your panties."

"Why Daddy?"

"I need you to take your panties off, and get up on this bed, so I can taste you down there."

"Daddy… you know we ain't supposed to have nothing touch our private parts."

"It's okay if it's me, Olivia. I'm your daddy."

"No daddy."

"Olivia…we keep this little secret now, you get that nice dress. You want that nice dress, don't ya girl?"

Olivia sits on the idea a beat. She knows the right answer here. She also knows the pressure. But this is a moment. "No, daddy no!"

Eddie, more commanding, "Now, just take off those panties, girl."

Olivia repeating herself "No daddy. No"

Eddie's eyes change, and instantly, he gets angry, threatening, "Girl!"

"No"

Olivia stands there. Eddie regards her. The moment is still and violent. Olivia turns and walks out.

8

Olivia, Jennifer, and Dexter sit around Olivia's table. Jennifer and Dexter are silent in contemplation at the story Olivia just told them. They silently ponder. Jennifer looks at her bags, "I can't imagine."

Dexter exhales and then gets tense at knowing as much as he does and that such things exist. He moves uneasily around the room.

Olivia soothingly says, "It's okay."

Dexter, almost angry at Olivia, responds, "How is it okay? How are you okay with it?"

"Dexter...sit down sweetie..."

Dexter waits a second...then sits...frustrated.

Olivia looks Dexter up and down, "You're upset."

"Yes. I can't imagine anyone doing that...and then I can't imagine anyone doing that and someone being okay with it."

"Dexter, it's taken me many years to be okay with it...and really, even now, I am not completely okay with it. But I am at peace with it."

"How can you be at peace with a monster like that in your life?"

Olivia wanting Dexter to understand. "Oh Dexter...you haven't even heard the half of it, but this is the thing. After everything you will hear about my daddy, after even everything he has done, I still loved my daddy...he was my blood. I didn't trust him. I didn't like him, but he was my father. And so I have come to peace with that. That that was who he was. And what he did was awful...I still to this

day never once understood how one person can do all the evil that
he did…he was sick, you know? Sick in the mind. He had no regret
for what he done, no remorse…he was, what's the word for that…?"

Jennifer, jumping in, says, "A sociopath?"

"Yeah…a sociopath. He didn't care about nothing but himself. He
did awful things to me, my family, and most of all to Diane…but he
was still my blood. So I found my peace…because if I can't find the
way to have peace with what he's done, then how can I have peace
and love of myself? We share the same blood."

Jennifer and Dexter let it sink in. Dexter finds his feet again.

Jennifer, wondering, asks, "Olivia…was school a place where you
found peace in your life?"

"No, Jennifer… not right away, anyway…when I was older,
yeah…in high school. But when I was in elementary school, I was in
a daze. I would be so miserable in school. I would just sit and stare at
the teachers and the students. I don't know if it was clothes, because
we were always looked so poor and miserable, or what…but school
could be just miserable at times."

Olivia goes on to tell Jennifer and Dexter how there were many
times when she was in class and she would just sit and stare with her
mind lost.

***

The name of the school is Wallace Elementary. It is the middle of the
day and Olivia is sitting amongst her classmates. She is older now.
Nine years old and still growing everyday. Her hair is long, black, and
wavy and her facial features are maturing into that of a young woman.
Although, she still likes to escape her present life.

She is just staring. The class is attentive and quiet. A teacher,
Miss Baxter, is standing at the front of the class. "Now, when we add
fractions, remember you must have a common denominator before
you can add the numerators. So let's look at an example."

Miss Baxter goes to the blackboard to write a math problem as Devon in the row behind Olivia is making a spitball. When Miss Baxter's head is turned and writing on the board, Devon puts the spitball in his mouth, gets it nice and wet and then pulls out a straw from his pants pocket. He loads up his straw. Olivia just maintains her stare. Miss Baxter turns back to the class. Devon looks as attentive as everyone else but Olivia, however, doesn't seem to be following along. "Miss Olivia? What I just say?"

The class snickers. Olivia snaps back into it. "I…I am not sure Miss Baxter."

"You keep your eyes on the board young lady."

"Yes Miss Baxter."

Miss Baxter returns to working on the problem and Olivia keeps her attention to the blackboard. Devon slowly brings out the straw as his fellow classmates watch in anticipation. He shoots, and then throws the straw under Olivia's desk and the spitball claps against the blackboard after whizzing pass Miss Baxter. Miss Baxter snaps to the class, "Who!"

Devon interrupting "It was Olivia Miss Baxter."

Miss Baxter reaches down at Olivia's desk and picks up the straw. "Olivia, you go in the back corner and you face that corner and you think about what you have done."

"But Miss Baxter."

The class chortles at the miserable plea from Olivia.

Miss Baxter stomps her foot on the ground. "To. The. Corner! And you all shut it tight."

Olivia walks to the corner and whimpers, holding back a full bodied cry as she hears the whispers of her classmates as she walks to the back of the room.

Later that day, Olivia was sitting in another one of her teacher's classes. Staring out the window as Miss Walters drones on in the background. The ground is muddy and cold with a late fall. Leaves litter the ground and the winter chill is evident. Outside, a zephyr kicks up a yellow leaf, and plays with it. It slowly dances in the wind. Olivia stares and a smile grows on her face.

The scene outside morphs into winter…cold, hard, and lifeless. The ground is covered in ice. The trees, stripped of their leaves, lightly move, active, personified, as if they are talking and moving in conversation to each other. The music, jazz, is now a soulful interplay of instruments that mimics the movement. Then, the music blending with the conversation of the classroom behind her, Olivia stares and watches. The classroom behind her begins to break loose as Miss Walker brings the class ready for lunch. Olivia turns her head as she hears the class room change. The music changes…a violin, it is slow and drawn out, teasing tension into the room.

"Alright class, let's put away your composition books." Miss Walker says as she looks across the room as the children silently follow her instructions.

"Good. Now, let's all line up for lunch."

Miss Walker looks at her grade book. "Olivia Clark."

"Yes…Miss Walker."

"Today, you are the Engine."

Miss Walker walks to the door of the classroom as Olivia slowly emerges from behind her seat, and takes the first position at the door to leave the classroom.

Miss Walker, still eyeing the classroom and smiling at Olivia, "Alright. The rest of you angels can line up now."

The class breaks out of their seats. Miss Walker watches them patiently.

"Alright, now let's all wait patiently for the bell."

Miss Walker turned to face the door and opens it. The hallway is dead silent, and the classroom feels emptier for it. Two kids in line behind Olivia are Clarence, an innocent young boy, and Terrel, a not so innocent young boy. Terrel leans forwards and speaks into Clarence's ear. Clarence hesitates, then Terrel whispers something else and Clarence realizes he has no choice. He reaches forward and pushes the girl in front of him, Ella. Ella falls forward into Olivia who falls into Miss Walker who almost falls into the door frame. The kids all laugh. Like a startled dog, Miss Walker whips around and smacks Olivia hard in the face, dropping her in heap to the floor. The act is so violent the class stops laughing immediately. Olivia takes a beat, then fighting tears, keeps her eyes downcast, fearful of a reprise, and stands. "I…I'm sorry Miss Walker."

Miss Walker readjusts herself. There is no initial remorse here… but at Olivia's words, see's what she has done and kneels down. She goes to put a hand on Olivia's face, where she hit her but Olivia flinches away. Miss Walker still extending her hand to Olivia's cheek "It's okay…It's okay."

The school bell rings.

Miss Walker looks at Olivia's face. She is regretful and tender. She stands and gently encourages Olivia to the side. "Step over here sweetie. Ella…you be the Engine today. Class…I'll meet you down in the lunchroom."

Miss Walker and Olivia watch the class leave in a patient clip. For Olivia, the memory of the incident washed away almost instantly. Olivia, still tears on her face, uncomfortable at Miss Walker's hand on her back, stands impatiently. The kids leave the classroom, and Miss Walker, who now has a tear in her eye, looks down at Olivia. "I think we'll have lunch together today. That sound okay?"

Olivia nods to Miss Walker. There is a genuine warmth in Miss Walker that seems to loosen Olivia. Miss Walker walks to her desk and opens a drawer to take out a coloring book and a new box of crayons. "Tell you what…I'm gonna go get us lunch. And you…I want you to color in this brand new coloring book I just received… and look…I have a nice new box of crayons to go with it. That sound okay to you?"

Olivia again nods with the hint of a smile. Miss Walker takes the coloring book and crayons over to Olivia's desk and sits them down. Olivia does not move.

"Olivia…It's Okay. Come on over. You color and I'll go get us some lunch."

Miss Walker grabs her purse at her desk and then heads to the classroom door. Olivia doesn't move. Miss Walker stops at the classroom door and turns back…sees Olivia staring at her desk, not sure of what to do. "Sweetie…it's okay. No one is going to hurt you here. I promise. I'll be back in a little bit with lunch…you color now."

Olivia watches Miss Walker close the door, then she turns and looks at her desk. The new coloring book and crayons look suddenly so unreal. She walks to them with reverence and gently slides into her desk so as not to disrupt them. She puts her hand gently on the crayons, feeling the crisp edges. The box is upside down as she plays with the opening flap, almost edging it out, then stops. She pulls her hand back, stares down at the crayons, then gives up. She turns her head outside, but now, the trees don't move. There is no music, and she just stares.

***

Olivia is still telling her life story in her living room. "I never told my parents or anyone what Miss Walker did to me. Often as a child, we didn't tell our parents when bad things happened to us because they would say it was our fault and beat us again. So from that day on, every couple of days, we would have lunch together. She would bring me all kinds of pretty paper dolls and coloring books…and eventually I even started allowing myself to color in them, ya know. She knew exactly how to treat me. She could tell."

Jennifer amazed at the stories Olivia is telling about her life, "She could tell what?"

"That I was abused. I think she knew…not the moment she hit me…that she did because I reckon she was abused too. But in that moment, when I stood up…and apologized…she knew."

"How do you know that?"

"Cause she saw herself in me. It's something you find out, when you been abused, that you can find others that been too…if you take the time to look. She never took the time to look, but she knew… somehow, she knew 'cause she let me look out that window. But she never saw me until she hit me."

Jennifer, a little puzzled, "So you can tell who's been abused?"

"I ain't no psychic, if that's what you getting at…but, when you been hurt, threatened, tortured…you know what fear is, what it's like to live with it. It's not just fear now, its panic at every moment. When you are sitting on the edge of a knife, just balancing…and that blade is in the hands of whoever it is…and you just hope and pray that they don't wiggle it just a bit. That you don't ever give them a reason to… that panic, that you might inspire them at any given moment…that's a fear you can see in others…if you know where to look."

"Where do you see it?"

"I see it in their eyes. Always in their eyes."

"And what do you see there?"

Olivia, looking past Jennifer in deep thought, "Sadness. We all lost our youth. And we are sad…that we never had it."

"Were there ever good times? Ever? Moments when being a child wasn't filled with fear?"

"Not really. There were times that we would do something that Daddy would say is special…like we would all get into the car and just drive down Hammond Road. Just drive…and look at the farms…but we never lost the veil of fear…something always brought us back…"

***

The family is loaded up. Eddie and Tiny sit in the front seat with Eddie Jr. between them. The rest of the kids sit in the back. Olivia sits by the window, looking out at the farms. It's the late 1940s and the kids are growing and understanding the words of every song they hear.

Motown music plays on the radio. Traffic runs by in spurts. Eddie drives with pride, and Tiny looks relaxed. The car is silent, but peaceful.

Olivia watches, and sees some cows. Olivia turns quietly to Diane who is next to her. "Diane…look. Cows!"

Diane, with her head down, "I don't care."

"Why not? What's the matter?"

Diane turns her head up to look at Olivia, and she stares at her. Her eyes are tired, fearful, and tense. She just wants to do nothing. Olivia stares back at her. Any excitement she had about the cows is now gone. They look at each other. Diane breaks the stare and regards her shoes instead. Olivia looks at her, then back to the road, her expression now plain.

Diane always has fear in her eyes. All the kids almost always do, but there would be moments, like on those drives, when they would forget how to be afraid…maybe just for a second…but Diane…she never does.

After the long drive, Eddie drops off Tiny and the boys at home so Tiny can get dinner started and the boys can toss around the football in the backyard. Diane is still regarding her shoes during the car ride and her fingers are playing at her dress. She hates those drives…and that car of his. Nothing her siblings did could ever erase that fear.

The dress that Diane has on is a tired, yellow dress. She is made up, prettier than normal…but now in the seat behind the driver. Next to the window, she still looks at her shoes. The car is still and quiet. Their cousin, Sunny, is in the middle and Olivia sits behind the passenger seat. They are driving again. This time, there is no lightness. Eddie's in the front seat alone.

During that summer, their cousin Sunny came up from the south to spend the summer months with them. Eddie would start to take them out on special trips where they would take long drives to Russell Island.

One time, Eddie drives over the Russell Island Bridge. The cars are actively moving around the majestic isle. It's a little eden outside of the city that looms to its north. The isle is trapped in a time of Dixieland music, picnics, and slow summers.

While slowly arriving onto the island, Sunny is craning over Olivia's lap as they look out at the life on the isle. Families picnic beside the water fountain, and music plays from the clam shell.

Sunny looking at the water, "Oh…are we gonna go swimming? I didn't bring my swim suit. What we gonna do if we go swimming Olivia? Uncle Eddie…"

Eddie sternly responding, "We ain't going swimming."

Olivia gave Sunny a look that says, "Stop talking," but Sunny is oblivious.

"Olivia…what are we gonna do here? Maybe, we will go listen to the music? That sounds like a…"

Eddie snapping back at Sunny, "Girl! You shut your mouth or I'll shut it up for you!"

Sunny has no problem interpreting the intensity of Eddie's threat. She quiets right down and sit in her place. The car drives around the island, heading deeper into a forest that dominates the south central part of the island. "You all sit in the car and shut up and you might get something out of it" Eddie says as he focuses on driving the dirt road.

Sunny looks like it could be a big deal, but Olivia knows otherwise.

The car continues on…driving deeper into the forest area until Eddie finds a parking place that's covered by a willow tree. A dark and shaded area where the car can sit. As he pulls up, a darkened path into the forest is apparent over his shoulder as he turns the car off, reaches into the front seat where he has kept his shotgun, then exits the car. He goes around and opens the driver's side backdoor of the car. Eddie looking to Diane "Come on, girl."

Diane hesitates and holds just for a second. Her sister and Sunny realize she has been crying.

"Come on girl…I ain't got all day."

Eddie takes the tip of the gun and caresses Diane's knee with it. He is stern and cruel, but the gun moves with a perverse sensuality up her leg.

"Now." He says as he looks around to make sure they are not seen.

Diane, head dropped to Eddie, slowly emerges. She stands next to him, facing the woods. Eddie addresses Olivia and Sunny "You all stay there. Not a peep, ya hear me."

Sunny and Olivia both nod…both in fear now. They look at Diane, her back still turned, and wonder as Eddie closes the door to the car, eyeing the girls in the backseat until it clamps shut. He moves next to Diane, puts his free arm over her shoulder, caressing her skin, sliding his arm underneath the strap of her dress, and then leads her into the forest with his gun at his side.

The girls sit in the car in silence. They hear no sounds, just their breathing. Their soft, subtle panic rises as Sunny slides closer to Olivia, both afraid to raise their voice. The island darkens as the sun moves behind a cloud, and they are shrouded in darkness. Sunny reaches for Olivia's hand, which is still. Sunny grabs her hand tight, wanting a reaction from Olivia, but Olivia's hand is just still, not reacting. Sunny whispers, "Olivia…hold my hand!"

Olivia looks straight ahead. There are tears in her eyes and she is crying hysterically, but makes no sound, nor moves an inch.

"Olivia!"

Olivia turns to Sunny in a snap – fear amidst her tears. "You be quiet, Sunny, so daddy won't hear us crying."

Olivia returns to her blank crying stare and Sunny retreats. She holds Olivia's hand like it's a teddy bear, stares straight ahead, and begins to cry. Sunny's crying is natural and normal.

Olivia still staring straight ahead. "Be quiet, Sunny. Please."

Sunny understands the fear in Olivia's voice is unmistakable. Sunny forces the silence into her cry. She looks down at Olivia's hand…lifeless in her lap.

Outside, there is also silence. The sun emerges from behind the cloud and the car lightens. Draped in shadowy tendrils from the willow, the car looks as if it is bathed in chains.

From behind the car, hardly noticeable, Diane emerges from the forest. She is not running, but moving quickly and awkwardly. She hurriedly grabs the car door, forces it open, sits, then slams the door and buries herself against it. Her hands, smeared with blood and semen, fall into her lap while holding a mangled up dollar bill. She is crying silently.

Sunny stares at Diane. Her crying becomes natural and unrestrained again. She cannot believe what she sees next to her. "Diane...What happened?"

Olivia, now alive, grabs her hand and forces Sunny around to look at her. "Shut up!"

The front driver door suddenly flies open. Olivia pushes Sunny next to her. Eddie throws the shotgun across the front seat. His shirt is untucked and he moves slowly into his seat. Without looking back, he starts the car. Coltrane plays a long mournful note as the cars moves away.

***

Jennifer, Dexter, and Olivia all sit silently. The unknown act, the abuse of Diane, and its unknown quantity freezes them to ponder. The air is heavy.

Olivia shakes her head, washing away the memory for a moment. "That day on...even Sunny had the look. It don't have to be you for it to abuse your soul."

Jennifer taken back. "Where is he now?"

"My father?"

Jennifer nods.

"He's dead. He was found murdered in his apartment. Been shot several times...We never found out who did it. He had so many enemies."

Jennifer can't believe it. The family…the turmoil. She stares in disbelief.

Olivia carries on with her story. "The boys never forgave my father. They always was getting some sort of a beating or another when they were young."

As Olivia replays stories of the boys being beaten, a montage of scenes plays out. "That old garden hose… he would just whip on them, senseless. He would just enter a trance, and just wouldn't stop… Daddy was always beating on Jake, throwing him to the ground, pulling up his shirt, taking out the garden hose and laying into Jake with recklessness.

One time, when Eddie Jr. returned from his paper route just 20 minutes late when he was out making money for us, daddy just took him and threw him into the stove, like a doll."

***

Olivia and Diane are sitting on the front steps of their house, looking out at the neighborhood, watching for Eddie Jr. From the side, they see him, pounding on the pedals of his bicycle, his empty newspaper bag wiggling behind him. He screams to halt in front of the house. Olivia and Diane stand up as he at first runs, then stops suddenly at the steps. He looks up at them and they look down at him. No one needs to say anything. Eddie Jr. looks down at his feet, then forces them upwards. He walks between Olivia and Diane and into the front door.

As Eddie Jr. walks in through the open door, he turns towards the kitchen to the right of the entry, hoping he has snuck in the home, and might not get caught being late. Eddie steps from behind the kitchen wall, stopping Eddie Jr. He looks up to him. "Dad…"

Eddie grabs nine year old Eddie Jr. by the shirt collar, lifts him effortlessly and throws him incredibly hard, twisting in the air, turning so that Eddie Jr.'s head collides with the edge of the stove. He drops instantly to the floor.

Eddie watches him fall, regards Eddie Jr., sees his chest heavy with breathing, and then walks over to his son. He witnesses the growing grotesque quality of Eddie Jr.'s injured eye, takes the money he still has clutched in his hands from his paper route, and walks out of the kitchen. Finally, he leaves the house. "I'm going out."

Olivia and Diane rush into the house, along with Tiny who enters from another room to tend to Eddie Jr.

***

Olivia continues with her story as they sit in her living room. "After all that, I guess they never could find the way to forgive him. They never could trust that it would all work out. I wish they would have."

Jennifer is upset. "That what would all work out? I don't…you sound like you are disappointed that your father is dead…but he, he was a monster. How can I sit here, and hear what you have said for the first time, to hardly know you, and to want this man dead… and you who have every reason in the world to…you sound like you forgive him…you sound…"

"I do forgive him."

"But how? How can you forgive such…evil?"

"I don't know if I will be able to convince you how…I am not sure why I am able to…cause you are right. I should want him dead…I should want to have killed him…maybe that's so…that is what is in my blood. My family has blood and violence strung all through it…"

Olivia pauses…gets up and walks to a picture of Tiny and Eddie from later in their life. She picks it up and looks at them. They are frozen in the moment. Eddie is looking down, a smile on his face and a beer held at his lap. Tiny sits next to him with a beer at her lips. They look peacefully apart.

"My momma always had two things…she had her beer. Especially as she got older, every day, she had a beer. A life filled with such madness…she died because of that beer…that was her way of escaping some other pain too."

Olivia turns back to the table and brings the picture to Jennifer and Dexter. "But she also had her scripture…and she had us know it too. From every day that I can remember, she would read to us from the bible, makes us read and memorize it back to her."

Olivia hands the picture to Jennifer, who looks at Olivia, than at the picture. "I'm sorry…"

Olivia with a heavy heart. "I think about it all the time. You see…it's all about trusting in the Lord…letting him take care of your sorrows. Of all the evil in your life so that you can simply love.

The summer that mom died of cancer was the worst day of my life. When the doctor told us she wasn't going to make it through the week, I said, 'Not my mom'. She was going to live forever. The doctor was right…I wanted to run into the streets and stop the cars because my mom just died. But the cars would just keep going. I felt so guilty because I was always in a hurry to get home to care for the kids. She deserved more of my time. I learned to talk to her in my quiet moments. It gave me peace about the whole situation."

Jennifer regards the picture. She sees just a man and woman. No evil. No monster. A moment frozen in time, that suddenly, slowly morphs to life. Eddie and Tiny sitting on the couch, laughing at a story being told around them. The feeling abounds of a warm family moment. They return back to the frozen picture and Jennifer looks up at Olivia.

Olivia, starting again, "Men always want to fix things…always want to mettle…so often struggle to have faith…to trust."

Jennifer wondering. "And Toby, my brother, couldn't trust?"

Olivia shakes her head. "Never could let go of the pain…wanted to make daddy pay for everything he did to us."

"Do you visit him? In prison?"

"Honey…when we are done here today…and you have heard all that I will have told you about my family…you tell me then if you would visit anyone in my family again. I want peace. I want love. I want to give…but they…well…I just can't."

Dexter wants to know more about Olivia's past and her family. "What happened with Diane? Is she still alive?"

"No…her life…gets even…well. Daddy, he never understood about being a woman. He always wanted himself one, or two or three for that matter…but he never understood us. When I was in junior high, and I was having my period ya know, well…we only had a few pairs of our underclothes 'cause we never got anything new. Always hand me downs or whatever we got from the Good Fellows. So I only had me three or four pairs of my personal items. So…I had to keep them clean when it was my time…"

***

Olivia is standing at the sink. She has a pair of underwear in her hands and she is washing the menstrual blood from her underwear. A pair of her now clean underwear hangs from a shower rod behind her. The room is bright white and the door is closed. Noticeably heavy steps occur outside the door. Olivia pauses…the water running over her hands as the footsteps stop instantly. She waits…her hand reaches for the faucet and touches the cold metal.

The doorknob turns and the door slowly opens. An intrigued Eddie sticks his head in. He is hoping to catch his daughter naked in the shower. When he sees Olivia with her hands covered in blood in the sink, he lunges at her, grabs her around the neck with both hands and chokes her. Slamming her head against the mirror behind the sink, lifting her up onto the sink, the water now pouring down her legs, onto the floor.

Eddie looks dead into her eyes with crazy rage.

Olivia is terrified. "No, Daddy! No!"

The door bursts open again as Tiny runs into and sees Eddie choking Olivia. "What in the Lord's name are you doing? She was just washing her private clothes…"

Eddie releases one hand from Olivia's neck and proceeds to wildly hit Tiny. The water becomes increasingly slippery on the floor, and handling the two women becomes an impossibility. Eddie releases Olivia who falls to the floor, in a puddle of water. She's breathing frantically to recover, blood mixing with the pool that rest beneath her cheek.

Olivia can hear Eddie shove Tiny into the hallway and he then storms down the hallway. Tiny enters the bathroom, bruised, bloody, and turns off the sink before helping Olivia to sit up.

Diane enters the bathroom. She is beautiful and elegant, but her expression is of anger. "What…Olivia…Momma…are you alright? What happened? What did Daddy do to?"

Tiny snaps at Diane and slaps her right across the face before Diane can finish the accusation of her father. Diane slowly turns back to Tiny with tears of surprise in her face, and they just stare at each other for a moment.

Tiny trying to cover her true feelings. "We are all right now. We just got to clean up is all. You go and take care of yourself."

"I just want to see if Olivia is ok."

Tiny smacks her again across her face. No anger in Tiny. Just putting a lid on the situation. "She's fine."

Diane does not stare back at Tiny, but drops her eyes and leaves. Tiny watches her go. Her eyes cold on Diane's back. Tiny turns to help Olivia collect herself and to help her clean up.

Diane enters the girls' room, eyes downcast like they just were, her face fresh from being slapped by Tiny. She moves to the small mirror that sits in one small corner of the room, where a miniature dresser with minimal makeup sits. Diane turns to herself in the mirror. She is truly beautiful, but the tears from her eyes, the red marks, and the pain in her face paint another picture in the dark and bleak room.

Slowly, she applies some make-up to her face and she begins to recover. Her shoulders relax as her beauty rematerializes in the mirror. She smiles artificially at herself, but at least she is transformed. Diane turns from the mirror and walks out of the room.

Tiny and Olivia finish cleaning up the bathroom and finish cleaning up her underclothes. Olivia's blouse is off and she is scrubbing with a ratty toothbrush to clean up the blood from her clothes. Tiny steps out of the bathroom then returns with some make up. "Come here girl."

Olivia goes to Tiny, who looks at her face. There is a small mark where she hit her head when she fell off the sink. Tiny takes a little make-up to it to help it disappear.

Tiny talking softly almost to herself. "Sometimes, we gotta do something a little special…"

She pauses as she regards Olivia. "I need you to go to the store for me. Need some sugar for tomorrow's supper. You do that for me?"

Olivia nods.

"Good. You change and get right on back. I'll put your blouse out back to dry."

Tiny turns her eyes away from Olivia to the pocket of her dress and gives her a quarter. Olivia holds it, takes it and feels the metal. Tiny turns to go out. "Don't you dawdle now."

The fear is back in Olivia…in that instant…in that threat. She moves to go out.

Olivia walks along the sidewalk along the projects. She moves simply, directionally, yet attracted by what she sees. The scene is silent and different from the row houses she lived in when she was younger but for the amplified sounds attached to the direction of her eyes. A bird, picking at garbage, flutters off. An old yellow car rattles by. She hears only what she sees. Her eyes are never fully on where she is headed, though her feet move her there unquestioningly. Her eyes move over the world, searching for beauty, searching…

Olivia turns down an alley, where the projects start to give way to a small industrial area that lies parallel to the train tracks. Those tracks divide Olivia's neighborhood from the city street just a half block away.

She crosses the tracks, and sees the back of Wilson's Grocery, where a small table sits outside and an open screen door gives a view inside. Inside the store, a young man named Sir Wilson sits at a table while talking to someone else Olivia can't clearly see. A fun Motown song called 'Dancing in the Street to the Beat' plays from a radio that sits on the table. Olivia stares at the man and the hidden person he is talking to. She hears a woman's laugh and wonders if she can recognize it.

Olivia emerges from the alley onto the city street, and turns to face Wilson's Grocery before eventually entering it. A few girls are in the back aisle. These are the girls talking to Sir Wilson through the backdoor. Olivia periodically peaks down the back aisle as she walks into the store.

Olivia's senses changes as she enters. She feels the eyes of everyone around her. The shopkeeper, Mr. Wilson who is a black, older man, watches her from behind the counter. The few patrons eye her as she walks through, and look at her with disdain. She looks slovenly, and acts downcast and trodden. There is no sympathy here...not in their eyes.

Olivia finds the sugar, takes it to the counter, sets it down without looking at Mr. Wilson, and then, peaks again down the back aisle.

Mr. Wilson is kinder than she perceived him to be. "Need anything else girl?"

Olivia not looking up. "No sir."

Mr. Wilson slides her the change. Olivia counts it carefully. Everything must be accounted for. He puts the sugar in the bag and regards her for a second. He reaches into a display of candy on the counter and hands Olivia a piece of chocolate. Olivia looks up at him.

"My treat."

Olivia, underneath her breath, says "Thank you, Sir."

Mr. Wilson smiles as Olivia's eyes return to her shoes. She receives the bag of sugar and walks quickly out of the store. She turns to the side of the store, puts the sugar under her arm, and takes out the chocolate to madly devour it. It's glorious, and she is starving.

Olivia puts the chocolate wrapper in her pocket and walks home. She moves past the outer wall of the store and follows the girls and Sir Wilson as they talk in the back of the building. There are large windows in the back of the building, so Olivia can continuously watch. Her eyes stay fixed on them, trying to decipher the conversation as she continues walking in the straight line home. She knows she recognizes one of the girls' voices but the chatter is so faint, she can hardly hear. Her feet negotiate the train tracks silently as her ears hear the conversation.

A mist of smoke and suddenly a train passes by, centimeters from behind Olivia. If she had walked even more slowly to try and hear the voices in the back aisle, that train might have actually hit her. The horn blaring and Olivia never hearing it for a moment because she is in a daze. She is wondering where the mist of smoke is coming from and what it could possibly mean. As the train races past, Olivia stands there with open and shocked eyes. They're still gazed on the back of the grocery store. The two women with Sir Wilson turn out to be Diane and her friend. They're all staring at her, now silent. Olivia holds the stare for a moment, then turns. It's best to head on home. She can't be late.

Diane yells, "Olivia!"

Olivia keeps walking. Diane runs up beside her. "Olivia! You okay?"

"Yeah."

"Hey…stop here for a second…"

Olivia knows she can't be late. "I can't."

Diane takes Olivia's shoulder, stops her and turns Olivia to face her. "…but you just been saved. You just been touched."

Olivia pauses. "I gotta go…we gotta go, Diane."

"I'll be there," Diane says as she reaches up to touch Olivia's face. "I'll be home soon."

Olivia turns and continues walking home, with a little more pep in her step, as Diane watches her from behind. Olivia doesn't want to be late. She hears nothing on her walk home. Her eyes stay to the path.

***

Jennifer, Dexter, and Diane all sit around the table listening to Olivia. Olivia looks out the window, watching the wind blow. "After that day…there have always been moments…times when I felt that God had reached down and plucked me…saved me…"

Dexter curious. "There were other times?"

"Lots of others…and after that moment I started to think back at times in my life that God had touched me…had saved me. He was always with me…"

Jennifer chiming in. "Like when your dad wanted to rape you in the bedroom?"

Olivia regards Jennifer's bluntness with surprise. "Yeah…moments like that. When I acted strong…those times, I realized when he was with me."

Jennifer geared up suddenly. "Olivia…"

Dexter, noticing the time, says, "Jennifer…we should go. It's getting late, and I think we've taken up enough of Olivia's time today."

Jennifer makes to argue, but looks at Olivia. She is haggard and drained.

Jennifer, a little disappointed because she wanted to hear more, responds, "Yeah. I guess so, but Olivia…"

"You two go and have a nice evening…but you come back tomorrow."

Dexter gets up and hugs Olivia. Jennifer stands up and watches the two. Dexter and Olivia release, and Olivia looks at Jennifer. Jennifer looks incredibly incongruous all of a sudden.

"Come here, honey." Olivia says as she reaches out to Jennifer and gives her a hug. Jennifer is uncomfortable at first, then relaxes as she feels the authenticity in Olivia's hug. "I'll see you tomorrow now."

Jennifer looks at Olivia for a bit, and then turns with Dexter and walks out the door.

They both walk to Jennifer's car. Jennifer clicks the automatic door opener on her SUV and the back trunk door opens immediately. She and Dexter set their stuff inside the trunk. Dexter goes to the front door, and Jennifer turns and looks at Olivia's house. She takes it in and is flat with affect.

9

Jennifer, Dexter, and Olivia sit around Olivia's back porch. It's a lovely day outside. Her porch looks out on a tired, tilting garage and a small, postage stamp backyard surrounded by a red picket fence. It's a pleasant space...tired, but welcoming. Olivia sits on an old wicker chair as Dexter and Jennifer share an old love seat.

Jennifer leans forward in a pause and then starts with her thought. "Olivia...before we...you...start again, I just want to say, that... well...That I am sorry...for everything...last night I couldn't stop thinking...not just how awful growing up must have been for you, but...well...that I was just so sorry that you, that anyone had to go through all that and that...well...I was sorry and also so appreciative, grateful, that you are willing to share with me...your amazing life."

Olivia regards her for a moment. It's a little heavy for an instant, then Olivia smiles considerately. "Now...I haven't always been able to talk about this, you understand. It's only in the last few years... been meeting with a doctor, a therapist, and we've been working on me. Trying to get me a little more comfortable with everything...with being me, and with being selfish sometimes..."

"What do you mean? Why do you need to be selfish?"

"Well...what we been figuring out...me and my doctor, is that I give too much of myself...anyone that needs something...my children, neighbors, family, even some woman up at the gas station who was asking for change…I just as soon give up the clothes I'm wearing than worry about if its freezing outside, ya know?"

Olivia pauses for a second and then continues, "I never had no joy when I was growing up…and if I can bring someone a smile, or something special…something better, well then I am happy with that."

Jennifer questions, "And sacrifice yourself? …"

Olivia nods, "mmm hmmm."

"I think that sounds like some good stuff to work on."

"Me too….now…where were we last night?"

"You were telling us about the train."

Olivia remembering, "Right. So not too long after that…I started in at high school, which for me…was one of the best times, one of the best places to be. Not only would I get breakfast and lunch every day, but I met my best friend, Marie, and we are still best friends to this day. In the lunch room, we would sit across from each other at a table of fellow students. We would talk like sisters and be in a world of our own. We would sit together every day…I would go to her house…we would laugh…It was like I had never laughed…we had such fun and I would look forward to going to that school every day."

Dexter with a questioning mind asks, "Why do I have the feelin' that that didn't last for long?"

"Oh…it lasted for me all through high school. I was always happy when I was at school and with Marie."

"But home?"

"Well…you know, Dexter. Things don't change. Sure…Diane was getting older…and hanging around boys, and she was always dressing and looking so fancy…she was always so lovely…you know she even did some modeling, but Daddy…he would still take her… still have her when he wanted. He was a monster."

Jennifer and Dexter look at each other…trying to imagine.

Olivia continues, "And then…when she was about 16 or 17, I think…everything changed…"

Jennifer wanting to know more asks, "She fight back?"

"Nope…she got pregnant."

"With…your daddy's baby? …"

Olivia just nods, "Yes…"

***

Olivia lies in bed. The room is dark. Diane's place next to her is empty. There's a light visible from the hallway, and the sink is distantly running. The sink turns off, and Diane returns to bed. She climbs in, and acts nauseous and uncomfortable. Olivia rolls over to her. "Diane…you okay?"

"Go to sleep Olivia."

Olivia rolls her back to her spot, but something is nagging at her. She rolls back. "What's the matter, Diane?"

Diane wanting to be left alone responds, "Olivia…"

Olivia wanting to help her sister pries, "Look…you tell me. You gotta tell me…I know there is something going on with you…you been acting funny…and you gotta tell me…we gotta tell each other everything…"

Diane turns to look at Olivia. "Okay. But look…you can't say nothin' alright."

Olivia nods.

"Not even to Marie, alright?" Diane pauses because of Olivia's reaction. "You gotta promise…"

"Alright…I promise…"

"I'm gonna runaway."

"Diane!"

Diane, fearful and looking at the door and then to Olivia, commands, "Hush!"

"But you can't…Daddy will kill you."

Diane with deep sorrow in her eyes says, "I gotta, Olivia."

"But daddy…he won't…"

Diane firmly states, "I gotta…I missed my time. I'm pregnant."

Olivia reacts with full depressing knowledge of what this means. She pulls back, but completely understands. Olivia rolls back over on her back.

After a second, Olivia questions, "When you gonna go?"

"I don't know…soon. Maybe tomorrow. I been talking to a boy, Phil, from school that got a brother with a car, about maybe getting a ride out of here, but I don't know if he's just trying to get me or what…"

Olivia turns back to Diane and moves to put her hand on Diane's belly. "What you gonna do with it?"

"I don't know."

They look at each other with shared misery. They hug, and then, both turn on their backs, looking at the dark, peeling ceiling. They reach out and hold each other's hands.

The next day, Olivia is sitting in front of the house on the step. The children are taking turns playing and riding on the family bike. Diane is noticeably absent. Olivia keeps looking down the street, hoping that Diane is coming home.

Olivia thought to herself that every day would be the day…and she would watch for her. And she would pray. Olivia prayed for Diane to get out of there…to fly away. She wasn't sure if she wanted her sister to have her baby or what…but Olivia just didn't want Diane hurt by their daddy no more.

As Olivia sits there thinking, Tiny opens the front door and barks at the children to come in for supper. Olivia looks down the street to her right, then her left, and then sees Diane with a small bump at her belly, hardly noticeable, but there, walking hastily to the house. A car drives by, and Diane gives the slightest wave to the young men sitting in the front seats of the car. She walks up the walkway as Olivia stares at the car that drives by. Diane walks by Olivia and into the house, as Olivia turns to watch her. Olivia reaches out and grabs Diane on the arm…instinctively, Olivia places her hand on Diane's belly. Diane turns, removes Olivia's hand, and shakes her head at Olivia, and then walks in. Olivia watches her go, and the door closes, leaving Olivia outside.

Olivia, again, thinks to herself about why her sister kept coming back. Maybe she was just getting' everything all ready to go, or she was scared, but she never told me nothing. But that's just as good as she just didn't want to get me in trouble.

10

A couple months passed and before anyone knows it, it is Halloween. Kids walk down the street in costumes, but Olivia and her fellow siblings just sit on the front porch, watching the kids go by. Most kids just past the house, knowing that there wasn't nothing there. A kid dressed as a ghost walks up the front path and Olivia just shakes her head at him. He stops...pauses, then turns around and heads back to the sidewalk.

Eddie comes out the front door with slacks, suspenders, and t-shirt. "All of ya get inside now."

All the kids obediently go inside. Olivia, the last one in, is grabbed by Eddie on the arm. He looks around at the porch. "Where's Diane?"

"I don't know. I haven't seen her all night."

"What you mean, girl?"

"I mean that I haven't seen her since I got home from school."

"You ain't lying to me are you, girl?"

"No sir."

Eddie getting frustrated shouts, "Tiny!"

"What?"

"Where Diane at?"

Tiny appears at the doorway and looks at Olivia. "I don't know." And then to Olivia, "Where's your sister?"

Olivia not knowing what to say "I..."

Eddie pushes Olivia inside the house. "You get inside." And then to Tiny, "Let's eat. I'll find that girl after supper."

Later that night, Olivia lies in bed, alone. She stares at the ceiling as she listens to the sounds of the house. A door slams and Olivia cranes to listen to the sounds outside the bedroom door.

Tiny, nervous, asks, "You found her?"

Eddie, even more frustrated, responds, "No."

"You ask up at the store?"

"Yea."

"Did you try over at the Mason's house?"

A loud smack is heard. "You stop your mindin'…get me a beer while I think this over."

Olivia smiles…hopeful…

The next day, Olivia goes through with a smile on her lips and she is happy…she is hopeful. Olivia is thinking to herself that Diane has made it. She thought about the wind blowin' through her hair and about her skin glistening in the sunlight…I thought that she'd be in the best of places. That she was free.

Olivia stares, still daydreaming about Diane…same expression from earlier. Then all of a sudden, she hears the door slam open. A ruckus. Olivia, bolts up in instant fear. She hears Eddie's voice. "Girl…now, you get yourself upstairs!"

Sounds of stairs and then Diane, tired, beaten, and bent over, walks and stumbles into the bedroom. Crying. She falls into bed.

Olivia worried asks, "Diane…what's the matter with you?"

"I don't know…"

"Well…what happened…?"

Diane just shakes her head…she can't speak, but she whimpers.

Olivia with growing concern shouts, "Diane!?"

Diane trying to gather herself to respond to her sister confesses, "Daddy took me to a doctor. Made me drink something." She moans with pain. "Oh…it hurts so much."

Olivia wipes Diane's sweaty brow and tends to her as a long night unfolds before them.

Later that same night, Olivia bursts open the door of Eddie and Tiny's bedroom. "MOMMA! There's something wrong with Diane… she bleeding!"

Tiny bolts upright and breaks past Olivia heading to her room. Eddie then rises. Olivia watches him, but she doesn't move. He walks towards her. "You be quiet girl. Let your brothers and sisters sleep."

Eddie walks ahead. Olivia follows him, but always behind him. They enter Olivia and Diane's room. The lights are on. Diane is sitting up at the head of the bed with her bedclothes pulled up around her waist. Tiny stands by her side. Diane's head is buried into Tiny's waist. Amidst the sheets of dark blood, a form appears, the aborted fetus from Diane's womb sits in a pool of dark blood and afterbirth. Eddie steps forward. He pulls the sheets forcefully from underneath Diane and wraps the fetus up.

Eddie turns with the bundle wrapped and held irreverently in his hands. He walks out the door and down the stairs. There is a silent pulse, but Olivia follows him, silently, behind…a ghost of a shadow. Eddie walks through the front of the house, to the kitchen, to the potbellied stove. He opens the stove and places the bundle on the top of the stove.

Without turning to Olivia, Eddie tells her to fill up the coal bin.

Olivia grabs the coal bin by the stove and then retreats outside.

She goes to a larger coal bin that sits next to the side of the house. She feels through the coal, sure to grab good, dry pieces. She then looks up at the sky. It is a clear sky with a moon that stands tall above, that slowly and suddenly fades into pitch black.

Olivia goes back into the kitchen and hands Eddie the coal bin. She watches Eddie from behind as he lights a match and places it in the coal pile at the bottom of the stove. The coal slowly ignites, then glows, and then turns into a turbulent fire in the furnace. Eddie grabs the bundle from the top of the stove and shoves it in amidst the pouring coals and closes the door shut.

Olivia watches as smoke rises from the stove and the heat pours from it. She breathes it in. The scent of flesh and blood causes her to retch. She steps forward, with bare hands that singe on the door of the stove, and she opens the door. The fetus lays there, unburned, in a raging fire of coal and flame. Olivia screams "Mommy help! Daddy is burning the baby in the stove". Tiny never answers because she knows if she tries to stop him, he will turn on her.

The next morning, Olivia awakes screaming, from sleeping on the couch. She is alone. The house is still and quiet. She ponders and shakes her head. "Was it...?"

Olivia quickly jumps from the couch, heads to the kitchen, and as she enters, she knows it's not. She smells the residue of the evening and notices a smear of blood on the top of the stove left over from the bundle. Still, she reaches toward the stove door. The door is still hot and she can't stand to touch it. She grabs the door hook, opens the door, and inside lies the charred baby fetus, dark soot against the white, still hot coals. Olivia slams the door. Her father stands in the doorway. He stares at her. Olivia stares back hard. She sets the door hook back, walks past him, runs up the stairs, and to her bedroom. She opens the door and Diane is lying there, sleeping, with Tiny by her side. Olivia makes to go in but Tiny shoos her out. Olivia just stares. She wants so much to be with Diane but Olivia had to obey ~~her~~ mom.

***

Jennifer has been noticeably crying. Olivia just stares at them as they sit across from her in the living room with mixed emotions on their faces.

Jennifer goes on to question, "How?"

Olivia stares at her. "That baby stayed in there for what seemed like months."

Jennifer covers her mouth just nauseous at the thought.

Olivia goes on to soften the dramatic length of the time frame. "Though I'm sure it must a been just a few days."

Dexter leans forward. "No one...removed...it?"

Olivia just shakes her head.

"I can't believe it."

Jennifer looks at Dexter. They share the horrible thought, and then both look at Olivia who stares out the window before them.

Her hands. Her skin. The years of abuse. Pain. Struggle and Survival. She is strong. Despite everything...as she stares out that window...she is soft, feminine and strong.

As Olivia looks out the window, she looks back on that horrible time that happened to Diane. "That was around 1953. I was just around fourteen and Diane was almost all done with high school. I helped take care of her when I could. She stayed sick for days after that. Daddy never even stopped in to see her and neither did Mom. I really believed Mom thought it was all Diane's fault. It was as if she wasn't even in the house."

***

Olivia sits at the side of the bed, taking care of Diane, wiping her brow. After about 10 days, she is finally well enough to get up and start moving.

Diane gingerly walks down the stairs as the family is gathered around the dinner table having a paltry meal. There is no open chair for her. Diane walks into the room and everyone in the family except Eddie stops eating and looks at her. Diane stops at the table, hungry, looks at the food. She was like a ghost moving through the house. Since Eddie wouldn't even acknowledge her, the kids hardly did either.

Olivia looks up at her, gestures and is about to say something...

"GIRL...keep your eyes on the food. Now, pass me them peas," Eddie says to Olivia as he slams his hand on the table. Olivia retreats her eyes back to the table and passes the plate of peas down so Eddie can have them. The family stutteringly returns to eating. Eddie keeps his eyes on his family, but never once looks at Diane.

Things with Diane changes after that time. She moves in and out of the house and Eddie hardly ever pays her no mind. It is like he thinks she is poison or something. Diane goes on to graduate from high school and is working up at the grocery store full time when she finishes up. She always spends her time up there, talking to the boys that worked there, and she hardly ever comes home before Olivia goes to bed.

One night, Olivia is lying in bed, staring up at the ceiling. It's dark. The house is quiet. Then, the soft turn of a doorknob is heard and gentle feet are climbing the stairs. The door to Olivia's room opens and Diane enters, and closes the door. She then gets into bed with Olivia. "Olivia? You asleep?"

Olivia, turning to Diane, says, "No...just watching the shadows. Where you been?"

"Up at the store with Fred and his friends. Just yacking and listenin' to music."

"Alright...good night then," Olivia says as she turns away from Diane.

Diane smiles and looks up at the ceiling. "Olivia...can you keep a secret?"

Olivia turns back to Diane. "What you think?"

Diane smiles, "Fred gonna marry me."

Olivia surprised "What?!"

"You heard me...gave me a ring and everything."

"Let me see it."

"I don't have it...but he showed it to me tonight...it was his momma's ring. He has to ask his Dad if it's alright...and then it's mine."

Olivia smiles and looks at Diane with envy, then asks the inevitable, "Diane...what Daddy gonna say?"

"Daddy ain't gonna be able to say nothing. Fred asked me and I said yes. We'll go up to city hall and get married, and then there is nothing he can do."

"Well…don't he have to ask Daddy for permission or something?"

Diane smirks, "Girl…don't be silly. That only happens in them movies. We are both adults and we can do what we want. Fred says he's got enough money for a wedding and for me to get a nice dress, and that will be that."

"When it all gonna happen?"

"As soon as Fred gets the ring I guess. I ain't gonna wear it until we are married. I don't want no one to know, ya hear me? You don't tell no one."

"I won't. Promise…I'm happy for you, Diane."

Olivia gives Diane a big hug and rests her head on Diane's shoulder.

***

Dexter and Jennifer are sitting around listening to Olivia.

"Amazingly enough…Diane was right. Fred had enough money for the wedding and her dress. Now it took a while before they were finally able to make it all happen, but one day they went down to City Hall and sure enough, they got married."

Jennifer, wanting to know more, asks, "And your dad?"

"Well…just like Diane said, there was nothing he could do. They come in one night. We had all just finished up dinner and I was in the kitchen with Mamma cleaning up the dishes. Daddy was upstairs when we hear Diane come busting in the door like she won the numbers or something…"

***

Olivia is in the kitchen with Tiny who has a cigarette dangling from her tired mouth. They both stand at the kitchen sink cleaning dishes.

As they work silently, they hear the front door bang open. Diane yells, "Momma!"

Tiny looks to Olivia. "You keep cleaning girl. I'll see what all this about."

Olivia keeps cleaning the dishes, but is intrigued by hearing Tiny from the other room. "Diane...what in the Lord's name...," Tiny begins to laugh, "Oh my...I just can't believe it..."

Olivia is too intrigued. She ponders a beat, then can't resist it. She puts the dishes down and walks out to the front of the house. Diane is lovely in a white dress that looks more like an evening gown than a wedding dress. She is beaming at her mother while standing next to a slightly nervous and equally smiling Fred who wears a nice but simple dark suit. Diane and Fred are both carrying some flowers. She is showing Tiny the ring and Diane sees Olivia emerge from the kitchen. "Olivia! Come here...we did it."

Olivia comes over and looks at the ring. Tiny is smiling. Olivia beams up at Diane and Fred.

Diane smiles, "Olivia...Momma...this...is my husband Fred."

Tiny, sharing her excitement, says, "Diane...we met before."

"But never as my husband."

"You have a point there...Fred..."

Fred gives Tiny a disarmingly honest, and genuinely sweet hug. He then gives her some flowers. "Mrs. Clark...I promise you that I will be a good husband to your beautiful daughter."

Tiny is genuinely touched. A tear forms in her eyes. Fred is honest and true, and Tiny can feel that. "That's good...you do that. She's my first baby...she deserves something special..."

Diane proudly says, "Momma...he knows...he already found us a nice apartment up on Outer Drive...one of those new buildings... everything's gonna be great..."

Diane continues her conversation with Tiny as Fred now moves over to Olivia smiling. "Olivia...I am looking forward to being your big brother. Sound good?"

Olivia smiles and nods, "Sounds good."

"Think you can introduce me to the rest of the family?"

"Yea! You bet." Olivia turns to the rest of the kids. "Jake."

Jake comes running over. He is younger than Olivia by a few years and looks wary.

Olivia looks up at Fred, "Mr..."

Fred smiles "My last name's Reynolds...but you can just call me Fred. We are family now after all."

Olivia smiles, "Fred, this is Jake, he's one of my younger brothers..."

Diane interrupts, "Daddy".

Eddie stands at the top of the stairs. He looms down on everyone, silent and cold.

Diane continues, "Daddy...we..."

Fred turns his attention from Olivia and Jake, and moves to join Diane by her side. "Mr. Eddie...I..."

Eddie begins to walk down stairs. He is dressed to go out. His demeanor and the look he gives to Fred quiets him just as much as Diane's hand clinching his arm. The whole house turns to watch as Eddie finished his descent. He eyes look up at Fred and Diane. "You got a place to live?"

Diane, starting to tremble a little, replies, "Yes, Daddy...Fred got a nice new apartment...over on..."

"When you movin' in?"

"Just after I get my things...?"

"Well, what's keepin' you?"

Eddie breaks his stare with Diane and she moves around him to go up the stairs. Then as she climbs up two steps, she turns back to Fred and Eddie. "I'll be right back Fred."

Eddie almost smiles, "He'll be fine. Now get on with it."

Diane runs up the stairs. Eddie and Fred hold the moment.

Fred holds his hand out. "Mr. Eddie...I just want..."

Eddie, just looking at his hand, says, "You gotta job right? Work up at the grocery store?"

"Yes sir...and Diane will too...just until my Dad retires here in the next few years and I take over...than Diane and I will have enough money so that she..."

"Alright."

Eddie pulls out a tired cigar from his inside jacket pocket. He puts it in his mouth and gives it a chew. He looks Fred up and down. He then says to Tiny without even looking at her, "I'm going out."

Eddie gestures for Fred to move out of his way and then walks straight out of the house. Fred looks at him as he walks out. There is a long pause. Then Diane rushes down the stairs...frantic...and panicking. "I'm back," she says as she tries to catch her breath. Diane looks around. "Where's Daddy?"

The room is quiet. Then Olivia speaks to break the silence. "He went out."

Diane a little shocked. "Out? That's it? ..."

Fred turns to Diane and takes the bag from her. "Yeah...that's it. Let's go home."

***

Olivia, Jennifer, and Dexter are in the kitchen now. Olivia is making a pot of tea as Dexter opens cabinets looking for something to eat. Jennifer is looking at him disapprovingly. As she waits for the water to boil, Olivia continues with her story.

"I graduated from Southwestern High School the next year and started working at Angel of Mercy Hospital as a nurse's assistant. See...I had told my momma that I wanted to be a nurse, but I knew she didn't have enough money to send me to school. I don't know how she knew him, but she called up Dr. Hanson King who was the owner and head doctor at Angel of Mercy Hospital. It was a black-owned hospital, and it was there that I started learning my trade. I left there after 3 years or so and moved to City Hospital, and then to Notak Hospital after that where I worked as a Nurse Tech."

Dexter, surprised, says, "I didn't know you were a nurse?"

"Well…I was laid off in the late 70's and haven't been back. So I don't know why you would know. Dexter…stop poking around my cabinets. What are you looking for?"

"I don't know…something to eat."

Olivia laughs, "Men are always hungry… My momma…ya know…she always had advice…and most of it was pretty damn good. The best advice she ever gave me about men was to always work to make sure they are happy when they get home. Make a good supper and even if you didn't have nothing ready or were too tired or what, to put an onion in the oven before they got home. So that when they walked in the door they could smell something cooking. 'Cause men is always hungry and they always want to feel like they're special."

"Olivia, I'm not always hungry."

Olivia, looking to Jennifer, says, "well…if they ain't hungry for one thing, they always hungry for something else…"

Dexter confused asks, "What do you mean?"

Olivia smiles, "You know what I mean, don't you Jennifer?"

Jennifer blushes but nods in agreement at Olivia's frankness. Dexter is still oblivious. "What?"

Jennifer chimes in, "Dexter…don't…"

Olivia, just being blunt, says, "If you ain't hungry for food, you hungry for sex."

Dexter just looks at her. The room is silent. Dexter has no idea what to say. Olivia looks at him and then starts to crack up laughing, "Dexter…you don't know what? …"

Dexter turns to the cabinet, embarrassed, "Olivia…stop it…"

Olivia laughs even harder at how uncomfortable she has made Dexter. Jennifer finds it infectious and starts to laugh as well.

Olivia, still laughing, continues, "The look on your face! Like you can't even talk about sex. What is it with men? They all want it… act like it's so important…but they can't handle talking about it…"

Dexter turns back to Olivia, then to Jennifer looking for some help. She smiles at him and turns to Olivia. "What other advice did your mother give you, Olivia?"

Olivia finishes up the tea, pours it into the tea kettle and grabs a sugar bowl. "Well, let's see…here honey, you take the sugar bowl…Dexter, grab us a few cups and follow us back out to the porch."

Olivia and Jennifer move from the kitchen to the porch, and Dexter is trailing with three tea cups and a box of graham crackers.

Olivia sits down and adjusts the throw pillow behind. She then continues on to answer Jennifer's question. "Now…another thing that Momma always told me was to always be the good wife. No matter how bad things got…no matter how bad your husband or your man was…to always be the good wife."

Jennifer curious asks, "Why was that?"

"because…if you went bad…if you were tempted to do just what he was doing…than nothing good would ever come…and you would be left with nothing."

"Do you think that is why she stayed with your father? 'Cause she was afraid of having nothing?"

"No…maybe that's what she told herself sometimes…that being with Eddie at least gave her something…but truth be told, she wasn't afraid of having nothing. She was afraid for her life…we all was afraid…that he would kill us. That's what kept her from leaving."

"Would he have killed her?"

Olivia looks at Jennifer. "How do you know he didn't?"

"I don't…Did he? …"

"No…but…honey…see my family…almost all…are…," Olivia repositions herself and sips her tea. "Maybe this will help…Diane and Fred, they'd been married about 2 years and things had fallen on tough times. Fred's dad not only gave Fred the store, but he decided to up and die on him before any of the legal…ya know…paper work could all be handled…and Fred, well he wasn't the best at running the business…he could never figure it out. So money got tight and they had to move out of the apartment. Daddy and Momma said they could live with us until things got better…that was the worst decision ever. Daddy never accepted Fred. Fred treated us like kings and queens and that angered Daddy…"

***

Diane and Fred are maneuvering through the house. Whenever Fred and Eddie are in the same room together, Fred and Diane are quiet and still. There is one time when Olivia, Diane, and Fred are sitting at the dinner table playing a game when Eddie walks in from being out. The house goes quiet and Olivia picks up the game and puts it away.

They all just tried to stay out of Eddie's way. And mostly, everything worked out alright. But while Diane and Fred were living there, other things returned to normal as well.

11

Jake and several of the kids sit in the living room. It's a cold, fall day outside. Wind blows the leaves around. Eddie walks in from the outside and a howling wind follows him as he closes the door. The sound of the shower from upstairs edges into the living room as the children fall silent on Eddie's entry.

Eddie looks around the room. "Who's takin a shower?"

Jake, speaking up, answers, "Diane…she came home from work early."

Eddie, looking at Jake, asks, "Momma at the store?"

"Mmm hmmm…"

"Stay down here, ya hear?"

Jake nods as Eddie moves upstairs.

Eddie walks up the stairs and down the dark hall way to the shower, where a bright yellow light shines from under the door. Eddie without any concern for being quiet, walks into the bathroom and pulls open the shower curtain, exposing Diane, naked and startled.

"What in…Daddy!" Diane is angry and shocked, but quickly becomes nervous and gives an artificial laugh "Daddy…what, why you being so silly…You can take a shower when I'm done…I'm a married woman…you shouldn't be in here…"

Eddie disregards her. He removes his sports jacket and hangs it on the back of the door. "You are gonna give me a little taste."

"Daddy…I ain't gonna do that to Fred…"

Eddie instantly hits her hard across the mouth. "Don't you say that name, girl!"

Eddie reaches over to turn off the water. "Now…you stand up… and let me have my taste."

Diane stands up, crying…tears cascading down her face, blood runs from her cheek. Eddie stands directly in front of her. Eddie takes his hands and begins raping Diane as he leans in and kisses her neck… his head and mouth move gently, but it is clear his hands are not. He kisses then bites at her breasts as she stands resolute…letting him rape her. His head drops below as he kneels down to orally rape Diane as she stands there…staring at her face in the mirror.

Eddie stands up and looks at her. "Still my little girl…now it's time to have your taste."

Eddie pushes Diane down to her knees.

Moments later, Eddie emerges from the bathroom with wet clothes in hand. Diane's sobs can be softly heard through the door. The shower starts up again as Eddie moves into his bedroom.

He raped her. No one knows how many times after Fred and Diane moved in but, her brothers and sisters hardly ever saw her in the house anymore…not without Fred being there.

A few days later, Olivia is sitting with Jake at the dinner table. Olivia is trying to help Jake with something as she gets dressed for work. Diane and Fred walk in from outside. Diane is carrying a bag of a few groceries. "Daddy's home?"

Olivia, responding to Diane but still helping Jake, "Yeah…he's upstairs. Taking a nap I think."

Diane looks to Fred, "Alright, I'll go put these away."

Fred walks over to Olivia and Jake. He looks at the schoolbook that Jake has in front of him. "What you working on?"

Olivia, knowing what they are doing, says, "Math…fractions… Jake's having a hard time, and I ain't no help…plus I gotta be going or I'll miss the bus…Jake…I'm sorry but…"

"Here…I can help you Jake…I used to be pretty good at fractions if I can remember…"

Olivia being thankful, says, "Ya don't mind?"

"Naw…sounds great…" Fred looks to Jake and asks, "don't ya think?"

Jake jokingly responds, "well…you can't do any worse…"

Olivia playfully whacks Jake upside the head, and smiles. "Now be nice. You know I never was great at math…"

Olivia turns over her shoulder toward the kitchen. "Momma! I'm going now…"

Diane and Tiny emerge from the kitchen. "Alright…what time you be home tonight?"

"I got the late shift, so about 3."

"Alright now…"

Olivia walks out as Fred sits down to help Jake, and Diane comes over behind him to watch for a moment. Tiny looks on. The family almost feels normal for a beat.

Olivia walks down the side walk to the corner, as the bus pulls up, she smiles, and the bus waits as she gets on.

Fred is sitting at the table now, helping Jake, and Diane moves to the kitchen to help Tiny.

"To multiply these guys, it's always best to turn the mixed number into a top heavy fraction."

Jake trying to get the hang of it says, "Like this?"

"Yeah…just like that. Now, you can cancel, and then multiply straight across just like the other ones." Fred watches Jake. "Yeah… that's perfect."

Footsteps can be heard in the near distance. Eddie emerges from the stairway and watches as Fred and Jake work at the table. Fred's arm is over Jake's back while he's crouched in and looking over the work.

Fred, encouraging Jake, says, "Great job…now let's try this one… same way…"

Eddie gets angry. "What the hell is going on here?"

Fred and Jake both turn to see Eddie stepping towards them.

"Mr. Eddie...I was just..."

"Dad...Fred...he was just helping me with my math."

Eddie grabs Fred, pulls him straight out of the chair, and throws him violently to the wall. Eddie has lost it. His eyes are mad. He holds Fred by the neck. Tiny and Diane come in from the kitchen and watch. "Who told you you could do that?"

"No one...he just needed some help....I'm sorry...I won't do it again..."

"Damn right."

Eddie throws Fred down to the floor and goes back upstairs quickly. Tiny watches Eddie as Diane goes to him on the floor. "Baby..."

Fred getting up says, "I'm okay...he just scaring me..."

Tiny looking up as if through the floorboards "No...you both gotta go..."

Fred confused, says, "What?"

Tiny, turning to Diane and Fred, repeats, "You gotta go now... he going to get his gun."

Diane understands this. Fred is hesitant. Diane is pulling Fred. "C'mon baby."

Diane grabs him by the arm. "We gotta go..."

"He's not gonna shoot me...he just wants to scare me..."

"No...you don't understand..."

"I was just helping Jake."

Tiny trying to get them to leave, shouts, "Fred, please! ..."

Eddie's steps suddenly come louder. He comes down the stairs with his gun in his hands. Fred moves to the bottom of the stairs, looks at Eddie and puts his hands up. With a look of belief that he might actually get shot, he pleads, "Mr. Eddie..."

Eddie fires a shot into Fred's left shoulder, spinning him around and down to the ground. He scurries up trying for the front door.

Diane yells, "Fred!"

Tiny grabs Diane by the arm "Diane…you gotta run! Go!"

Tiny grabs Diane as realization hits her. Tiny pushes her towards the kitchen, towards the side door to the house. Diane looks at Fred and then runs.

Fred gets up, moves towards the front door as Eddie shoots him in the back and lays him flat. Eddie unloads the shells from the gun and moves to stand over Fred. He loads two more shells in the gun before turning Fred over with his shoe. Eddie looks him in the eyes, and Fred struggles for life. "You ain't never gonna do that again."

Eddie puts the gun at Fred'S neck and pulls the trigger. An explosion of blood.

Diane runs, frantic and crying. As she hears the third shot, she falls and scrambles on the ground. She gets up and continues to run.

Eddie watches the blood run from Fred's neck in a dark river out the door. He turns to Tiny and points the gun at her. "Where's she?"

Tiny shakes her head. Eddie's eyes follow the path from the front room to the kitchen that Diane undoubtedly took. He calmly steps over Fred's body to the front porch. He looks down the street.

Eddie turns back to the front, and surveys the street. Nothing. No sign of her. He walks back to the front of the house. Steps through the blood that drains from Fred. Walks to a chair that sits on the front porch and sits with his gun across his lap. He takes the gun in his hands…he looks mad. He looks at the gun…holds the barrel so that it points at his head. Measures it out with his hand on the trigger and opens his mouth, tears flowing from his eyes.

Tiny calmly, says, "Eddie…"

Tiny kneels down next to Eddie and puts her hand on the gun. "Eddie…"

Tiny guides the gun so it lies flat, pointed away from both of them. She stands up and takes the gun inside the house. Eddie just sits there on the porch looking down the street.

Meanwhile, Olivia sits at a nurse's station at Burk Mercy Hospital while writing in a patient's file. She finishes, gets up, goes to a patient's room and puts the file in the file holder outside the door. She creeps into the room to check on the patient, an elderly man on a breathing machine. He is asleep; his breaths are irregular and painful. His blanket has fallen off of him. Olivia sneaks in and pulls the blanket over him. His eyes open and he looks at her with a smile in his eyes. She touches him with genuine love.

Olivia walks out of the patient room, goes down the hall to the closet, gets her coat and hat, puts them on, feeling good about the work she has done.

Olivia rides the bus, almost all alone, the driver and one other passenger in the back of the bus. She watches the street lights, and listens to the quiet of the late night city. She sees police lights in the distance. The bus gets progressively closer to them. She watches them. The bus stops.

The bus driver turns to Olivia. "Your stop ma'am."

Olivia is amazed…and instantly concerned. She gets up with her eyes following the lights. She walks, and then runs to the lights of her home. Tears begin as she fears the worse.

She moves to the house. A police car in front with Eddie in the back of the car, hands clearly handcuffed behind him. He watches her as she walks by the car. Her eyes turn to him. Olivia stops…jumps to the window and pounds on the glass. "Daddy, what did you do?"

She cries as he looks at her blankly. "What did you do?!"

A police officer comes over, helps pick up Olivia, and guides her to the house. Olivia fights over her shoulder yelling at Eddie.

Diane comes out of the house and walks up to Olivia and the officer. "Olivia…"

Olivia turns to Diane and embraces her "Diane! Is Momma…?"

"She's fine." Diane starts crying. "He shot Fred."

Olivia shocked "What? Why? Diane…"

"I don't know…but he's going…they gonna take him away."

Olivia pulls away from Diane. Diane just stares now at Eddie and he looks at her from the police car. They stare back at each other. "I hope they take him away forever."

Olivia looks at Diane and then walks into the house as Diane maintains her stare. She looks down at the outline of where Fred was, the blood still staining the porch and the walls. A few police move around the home, looking for evidence. A detective sits at the dining room table talking to Tiny. Olivia sees this all, it slows down…as if in a dream.

***

Olivia, Jennifer, and Dexter sit on the front porch.

Olivia continues with her story, "But he didn't go away forever. 7 years. That's all."

Jennifer, upset, responds, "For shooting Fred three times? That's ridiculous, and for no reason. All because he was helping Jake with his math."

Olivia nods.

"Why didn't he get more time? …I don't understand…"

Dexter, looking at Jennifer, says, "Jen…you would…you would if you were black…"

Jennifer is a little taken back. "What do you mean?"

"Things just work different…especially in this town. There are not tons of people in the system that fight for us to get justice…they just see it as a problem within the community…"

Olivia, looking at Dexter and Jennifer, agrees, "And they just let it go."

Jennifer, upset, remarks, "That's preposterous."

"That's life sweetie…that's how it all goes."

There is a pause in the conversation.

Jennifer, trying to understand, asks, "So…with your Dad gone…I assume things got better…that you were free…?"

For a little while. Diane went to go live at St. Lou's, where she worked in the rectory…learned how to cook…and just had a simple life…

***

Diane lives at St. Lou's where it's a simple life. She works, learns, and lives in simplicity, but she is not alive…she is just going through the motions.

Olivia is pretty much the same. Olivia goes through life…taking the bus, walking home, and helping with her brothers and sister. She talks to Tiny, and gets her beers. Tiny drinks herself numb.

Olivia has started to go out a bit more to have a bit of fun. She puts on makeup, dresses up a bit, and beautifies herself. There is a lightness to her step. She stares at herself for a beat in the mirror…she is happy with how she looks…a tear forms, just for a moment. She looks up to God…with a smile.

Afterward, she walks down the stairs, heads outside and smells the fresh air…she feels GOD everywhere…she runs out. She runs to the corner where her friend, Marie, picks her up in her car. Olivia hops in with a bounce no one has ever seen.

Later that night, Olivia and Marie walk into a place called City Club. Olivia is timid but comfortable. It is still a new world, but the place is hopping. "Baby, You Got Me" is playing and people are just digging the groove. Olivia walks in…her eyes wide and she falls in love with the rhythm and the energy of the night.

Olivia dances, the night has hazed, and she is reveling in it. She dances on her own…spinning…moving in synchronization to the music. A dancing man moves in and glides himself along with her. She is suddenly awoken to him and shocked, but he continues to dance and she allows his gentle touch to subdue her. She enjoys his gentle touch and begins to reciprocate. He wears a cross around his neck, is attractive, and kind. They dance romantic and charged, but still safe and appropriate. They share the rhythm of the music.

This is the first time that Olivia likes the touch of another man, while they are dancing and listening to the beautiful music. She almost forgets about everything…she almost lets it all go.

The last song is playing. The song is slow and rhythmic…just instruments. Olivia and her dance partner still are together while other dancers enjoy the music. His face is still darkened by the dim lights. The music collapses and the dancers leave the floor. Olivia holds the dancing man, but he turns to leave. She reaches out and holds his arm, not wanting to let the evening go. He looks at her and kisses her forehead. Her body instantly relaxes. Her arms drops, he pulls back from her and then walks away. Olivia stands in the middle of the dance floor and stares at the space he has left.

***

Olivia, Dexter, and Jennifer are on Olivia's back porch.

"I never saw him again…and I never danced with him again… we would go back…Marie and me…but never once…and I've wondered…"

Jennifer wants to know more. "Wondered what?"

Olivia smiles at Jennifer. "You ever have those moments… when you know you were a part of something special? Something beyond you?"

"I'm not sure…maybe. You mean…like at the train?"

Olivia smiles again and sips her drink. She sits there quietly… closes her eyes…playing the moment again in her mind and letting Jennifer and Dexter just sit. They look at her, then at each other… and eventually Jennifer asks the question. "Olivia?"

Olivia, eyes still closed, answers, "Yes dear."

"Did you ever marry?"

Olivia closes her eyes a little tighter, and gestures her hand to Jennifer to wait just one more moment. Olivia holds the moment, and then relaxes…just like with the dancing man. Then Olivia slowly opens her eyes. "Yes dear…I'm sorry…you asked…"

"If you ever married…"

Olivia reaches over to her side and picks up a framed picture of her with three children. "Well…of course I did…see…it's from my husband I got two of my three lovely children…"

Olivia hands Jennifer the picture frame. Jennifer holds the frame of the unassuming picture. Olivia and her three children sit uncomfortably on a couch, not looking at a camera, but eyes uncomfortably looking off to the side at something.

"The oldest, next to me, is Susan, then Willie. They were Frank and mine's, my husband. Then Carolyn, my youngest is from another father.

"Where are you looking in this picture…?"

"At my Daddy. That was from after Diane died, and he was at my home. I always kept my children with me when he came around. He was always after the girls…offering them money or to go for a ride with him. Daddy would walk behind me and say, 'Girl, you look beautiful. One day I'm going to grab you.' I finally asked him to stay away from my home.

I met Frank…well…at a gas station of all places. By then, I had started to have faith that maybe all men weren't like my Daddy…like the men in my family."

***

One summer at the neighborhood gas station, Olivia and Marie are walking by the gas station. A group of three men (Ronnie, Frank and another person) are in front. Frank is sitting down at a makeshift table, watching the world go by. They watch Olivia and Marie with mildly prurient interest.

Ronnie is not scared to say hi to the ladies. "Hey…honey girl…"

Olivia and Marie giggle, turn back and then keep walking.

"Honey girl…wait…we…we gotta question for ya…"

Marie turns to face the men. "And what question is that, Ronnie Johnson?"

"Sweet Marie? Is that you?...Come here honey...We, we gotta a question for you..."

Marie and Olivia walk over to them. Marie is the more aggressive one. She stands amidst the three men while Olivia stays to the periphery. Frank is shuffling cards on the low table, working on his three card money skills. He peeks at Olivia and she looks back at him. All throughout the conversation, Olivia and Frank steal moments with each other.

"Alright...here I am. What's your question, Ronnie? 'Cause if it's to ask me out again...well, you can just kiss that idea goodbye."

"What? No...and why do you say that honey pie? Didn't I treat you well last time...?"

"If you call sitting with your Mamma while she had you clean the mess you made in her basement, then no. I ain't going out with no boy who don't respect his Mamma."

Ronnie looks indignant as the men laugh. "Now alright...but we had a nice time after that right...up at Charlies?"

"Was that before or after you started talkin' to the hoochie at the bar?"

The men laugh at this even more.

"Well...a man gotta keep his options open don't he?"

Marie with a look "Let's go Olivia. There ain't nothing here for us, that's for sure."

Marie walks on and Olivia follows. Frank gets up from his table, and jogs over to Olivia and Marie. "Excuse me..."

Marie, turning harshly around, shouts, "What you want?!"

Frank, looking at Olivia, says, "I...was wondering...what's your name?"

Getting butterflies, she answers, "I'm Olivia".

Frank speaks with a genuine drawl that is patient and honest. "Olivia...that's a really pretty name...for a really pretty girl."

Marie, fed up and getting impatient, insists, "Oh dear...Olivia... let's go."

Marie walks on, and Olivia feels pulled in two directions.

"Hey" Frank lassoing Olivia for one more moment, but he knows it's fleeting. "You live around here?"

"mmm hmmm."

"you think…maybe you could come by again some other time… and if I'm here…maybe…we could find some time for each other someday?"

Olivia smiles, "Yeah…I think I can do that."

"Good. That would be real good."

Marie is getting more and more impatient. "OLIVIA! C'mon!"

Frank ignores her friend. "I look forward to it…Olivia."

Olivia gives him one more smile and then hurries to catch up with Marie. The two of them continue walking their way, and Marie wants Olivia to know how she feels. "What you doing getting all messed up with him now?"

"He was nice, Marie."

"He's a friend of Ronnie Johnson. That only means trouble."

"I liked the way he talked to me…all nice…and buttery…"

Marie gives Olivia a look. "What? Olivia are you serious?"

"He just warmed me up…ya know…I never felt that way about a guy before."

Marie laughs. "There ain't nothing but a boy talking to get in with you…but…if you wanna…that's all on you…"

"Yeah…I don't know…but maybe I do…"

"They keep walking for a minute. Then Marie stops and smiles at Olivia. I do like it when they talk all buttery."

Olivia agreeing "mmm hmmm".

They both laugh in acknowledgement and keep walking.

12

Two months later, Olivia, in a simple white dress, and Frank, in a nice suit, stand in front of the judge. Tiny is sitting in a chair while Diane stands next to Olivia, holding a simple bouquet of flowers. No one stands next to Frank. He looks terribly unrepresented.

After the wedding, Tiny has a little barbeque in her and Eddie's backyard for Frank and Olivia. Olivia's family is running around as Olivia, Tiny, and Diane set a table with four chairs. Olivia and Diane drink cold lemonade from glasses, and Tiny, a cold bottle of beer. Frank is playing baseball with Olivia's younger siblings as the women watch. Frank falls down trying to tag one of the kids...Olivia just laughs.

Diane, looking at her sister, says, "You might have found yourself a good man there little Olivia."

Olivia nods...she might have. Tiny however, does not look confident. "Olivia...you know what's about to happen now...right."

"Yeah Momma...I think I do..."

"That's what you think...but I ain't talking about what you do in the bedroom, girl...I'm talking about a man...he changes when he has you."

"You...you talkin' about Daddy?"

Tiny pauses. "Yeah...he changed...but I think I coulda saw it if I looked harder...I mighta saw what was coming for me...but I had

Diane. Not alotta men look at woman with a child…I think that I just felt so lucky that I chose not to see how he was gonna change.

Diane and Olivia take this in. Tiny is still as water, and the girls have never heard her be so candid.

"Your man…he gonna expect things of you. It's your job now that no matter what you want to do that you keep your man thinkin' that you always carin' for him. No matter what."

Tiny swigs that last drink of her beer and looks despondently down into the bottle and then back up to her girls. "You put an onion in the oven when you ain't got supper ready but he's about to be walkin' in the door. Men don't care that you had work or babies crawlin' all up and down on ya, he just wants to know where his supper at. And when he wants to be at you, you just let him have you. Ain't nothing good gonna come out of lockin' yourself up with a lock and key. Let him root around in ya…it's all they know."

Olivia looks at Tiny trying to understand. "Momma…I don't think…"

Tiny suddenly gets angry. "Don't you question me." Tiny stops to take a breath. "You'll find out soon enough now…now you go on… get me a sip now would ya?"

Olivia looks at her hands "Sure Momma…I'll go get you a sip…"

Tiny talking to Olivia as she walks away "Oh and Olivia. Since you've married him, your pillow will be wet every night…"

Diane watches as Olivia takes a slow, sad exit from the table and leaves, and then watches the party as Tiny looks at her bottle of beer. Diane reaches out with her hand to Tiny, who takes it just for a bit and holds it.

13

Olivia comes in from work. She's frantic. A small bag of groceries is in her arms, and she impatiently sets it down. She turns on the oven, then reaches to a floor cabinet, takes out an onion and lays it inside the oven door. She then changes her attention back to her groceries, and quickly puts them away. Then, she finds a left-over casserole in the refrigerator, and examines it. "It's enough for one person. It's dry and tired, but might do."

Olivia scrapes out the remnants of the casserole into a bowl, and begins to add a few other ingredients to make something come together. As the door opens behind her, Frank walks in. She scampers to look further along.

Olivia, turning to him, says, "Welcome home Frank…"

Frank gives her a nod, and walks past her, into the living room. "Bring me a beer now."

Frank takes off his jacket, visible through the cross slit in the doorway out of the kitchen. He hangs it up in the front closet, turns on the radio, sits down and unties his shoes. Olivia comes in with his beer, and waits for his shoes.

Frank not even looking at Olivia, "My supper ready?"

Olivia bends down to pick up his shoes and set them by the wall. "Soon…How was your day?", she says with a forced smile.

"Same. Filled with nothing...everywhere I go." Frank says as he looks at Olivia. Then she looks back at him...not sure what to say. "My supper? ..."

Olivia snaps out of her daze. "Yeah...just a little bit more...you relax...here before you know it."

Olivia scurries to the kitchen.

A few moments later, Frank is sitting in front of a plate and an empty casserole bowl. He is eating hungrily. Olivia sits next to him, nothing in front of her. Frank stops a beat suddenly. "Didn't we have this...what is this slop...chicken casserole...just the other day?"

Olivia looking down at the empty casserole bowl says, "I don't know...don't remember."

"You ain't feedin' me leftovers now are ya, girl?"

"You smelled me cookin' when you came in didn't you?"

Frank nods and returns to his dinner. He stops, looks up at Olivia and slaps her. "You remember what you makin' me for supper now. No more of this same dinner in a week, ya hear?"

Frank takes the last bite, cleans his plate and stands up. "Taste like shit anyway...why I marry such a lousy cook."

Olivia sits...watches him get up, turn the radio back on and sit down in his chair. She puts her hand to her cheek and touches where he slapped her. A tear finds the folds of her eye. Olivia thinks back to the day in her mom's backyard when she said her pillow would be wet every night. She was right. It was wet every morning, noon, and night. That was the only time she didn't take her advice.

Later that night, Olivia lies in bed. The light is on behind her. Frank is getting ready. Olivia lies there, back to the light and to Frank, trying to decipher what tonight will bring. The light turns off, and Olivia closes her eyes, trying to find sleep. Frank sits down on the edge of the bed, reaches over and turns Olivia over on her back. He forcefully rubs her breasts for a moment, then mounts on top of her. He has sex with her...rapes her. Olivia just lays there...takes it in, takes a deep breath. He never seems to stop...

The next morning, Olivia gets up while Frank is still asleep, showers and dresses for the day at the hospital. Quietly. Always looking over her shoulder, looking at Frank, hoping he doesn't wake up. She moves downstairs, makes him breakfast, then grabs an apple and walks out the door to go to the bus stop.

Olivia stands with a few other people at the stop. It's a cold, early winter morning, and everyone is bundled up. A steam vent pours into the street making punctuated blasts in the air. The bus emerges through the vapor.

Olivia walks in and sits next to a nice looking older woman in the seats that run the long side of the bus. Olivia is tired. Her face is swollen from Frank's slap and her eyes are tired from the stress of living with Frank. She puts her hand to her belly to feel her child. She is not showing, but the life is inside of her…she starts to cry.

A hand, from the older woman next to her, offers Olivia a handkerchief. She takes it and dabs at her eyes. "I'm sorry…"

The older woman leans in closer to Olivia. "Don't you worry, honey."

Olivia still wiping her eyes, responds, "Thank you."

"Problems with your husband?"

"No…Yeah…how'd you know?"

"Girl cries at night, there must be a thousand reasons…but a pretty girl like you crying in the morning…only one reason for that."

Olivia nods. "Guess that makes sense."

"I been doin' this a lot longer then you have sweetie…I got lots of sense. Just don't have much chance to use no more, that's all."

"Yeah…well…thank you…"

Olivia hands back the handkerchief. The woman takes it, folds it meticulously and returns it to her purse. "You're welcome…He know you're pregnant."

"Not yet."

The older woman pats Olivia on the leg and gives her a long glance. "I'm gonna tell you what you need to do…it's real simple… but it will change your life…you ready?"

Olivia just looks at the older woman. "Yeah…"

"There ain't no changin' no man…not once they got their teeth into ya…so tonight, you gonna smile, you gonna do everything you do that makes him happy, ya hear me?"

"Yea…but I ain't liking it…"

"Well…you will…cause see first…right when you get home, you get Bible…you get it out and you read it…and you let those words settle right into you."

Olivia stares out the window, then back at the older woman.

The older woman continues. "Every night…first thing when you get home…you read that Bible. Let HIM in…HE will protect you."

The older woman stares down at Olivia.

Olivia thinking about what the older woman just said. "I will."

"Good…I can tell."

The bus stops. Almost everyone gets up to go including Olivia, but the older woman does not. She reaches up and tugs at Olivia's coat. "HE's already touched you…you let HIM touch you again and again. Once you feel HIM every day, you won't be cryin' when you riding on the bus."

Olivia reaches her hand out and takes the older woman's hand in hers. "I will…thank you so much."

"You're welcome."

Olivia walks off the bus.

A few days later, Olivia walks in her and Frank's house with a bag of groceries, but not frantic this time. She sets it down, starts the oven, puts an onion in there, then leaves the kitchen. She goes over to a side table and picks up her bible, sits down and reads it. She reads it intently, closes it, and then smiles…

***

Jennifer, Olivia, and Dexter are still sitting on Olivia's back porch. Olivia sips her tea and then continues. "And so I did…every day. Every chance I got, I would read my Bible. Everything in my life became tolerable because I could always go back and feel GOD with me. I really didn't care anymore about my husband; what he was doing or not doing."

Jennifer reaches for her necklace, but doesn't take her eyes from Olivia. "Were there other moments? Like the train? Moments where you felt GOD?"

"Every time...every night as I read the bible...every time I said the psalms...yes...they kept me whole despite everything that happened..."

***

There is a party with lots of people. Music is playing, and the atmosphere is fun and jovial. People are dancing, hooking up, and having a great time.

One of the people at this party is Frank. He is talking and dancing with a young girl, May. They are close, talking, and sexual in their movement. May seems coy and maybe a little uncomfortable, but still used to Frank. "What's going on with you girl? How come you not moving with me..."

"I...I'm pregnant Frank..."

Frank steps back for a moment. "Me?"

May angrily answers, "Well, who the hell else? You been poking me every day for the past six months."

Frank likes this idea and moves in to take her close. "Good... that's why you looking so good to me now. I'm just gonna have to eat you up."

"How am I gonna..."

"Don't you worry...I'll take care of you...now shut up and start moving with me..."

May smiles, livens up, and digs into Frank. They move in rhythm and lust.

That same night, Olivia wakes up and looks up at the ceiling. Taking a deep breath with her hands to her belly, she is fully pregnant.

She turns and looks at the clock next to her bedside, 4:15am. She looks over to where Frank should be sleeping, but he is not there.

Olivia looks up to the ceiling and thinks to herself, "He ain't been working the night shift, so that must mean he fooling with another woman."

Suddenly, a smoky cloud, light and hardly there, clouds the ceiling. Olivia knows it's GOD's confirmation…and then the smoke disappears.

14

They attend a backyard party at someone's home in Washington. It's a warm, summer night, with cold beer, and music. Light and airy. Frank and Olivia, very pregnant, walk in from the driveway. They are apart as much as they are together. They smile and greet people. Frank grabs a beer from a cold bucket filled with ice.

As they move through the crowd, a woman is slowly revealed, May. She is equally as pregnant as Olivia. Frank goes over to her and too warmly hugs and kisses May. Olivia stares at May and May smiles at her with a knowingly arrogant smile. Olivia begins as if to cry, her eyes almost water and weakened, but then there is a little more smoke over Olivia's eyes. She knows it is GOD's wisdom and she feels strength. Olivia strongly smiles back, disarming May. Then, Olivia drops the smile and looks away as if May and Frank are not even there. She then walks away...

15

Years pass now and Olivia is stronger and more mature. She has two children and is cutting her youngest child, Frank Jr.'s, hair. There is a large afro style slowly diminishing as Olivia trims it. Hair falls to the ground, and Olivia keeps cutting as she sings a song.

Frank walks in with a little stagger as he is drunk. He looks up at Olivia and Frank Jr. "What the hell are you doing, woman?"

"What's it look like…I'm cutting your son's mess of a hair."

"Did I say you could do that?"

"No. I didn't think…"

Frank turns away. Frank Jr. looks up at Olivia, she nods and then he leaves.

Olivia talking to Frank "Frank…I'm sorry…I didn't know…"

Frank, turning back to Olivia, says, "You are a damn stupid fool."

"Frank…"

Olivia retreats as Frank aggressively runs after her. Olivia runs into the wall behind her and Frank sends a powerful punch at Olivia. In a smooth layer of smoke again, Olivia moves her head just in time, and Frank's hand powerfully collides with the wall behind her leaving a tremendous hole. Clearly, the punch might have killed her.

***

Jennifer upset says, "He coulda have killed you."

Olivia nods, "And he would have…had GOD not played a most curious hand in everything…most curious. The more I think about my family, and that I have survived the sense of it all…well there is only one reason why…GOD…"

Jennifer looks at Olivia with puzzlement. "What do you mean, Olivia?"

"Well…my Daddy…my family…you just wouldn't understand…"

***

Maggie, Olivia's sister, sits at a table in Olivia's dining room. Olivia is doing some sewing. She takes a long pair of scissors and cuts some thread. Maggie is holding Crystal, Olivia's baby, still and without love, just holding her. Olivia looks up to Maggie. "How's Momma?"

"Ya know…always drinking…she just been sitting around so much…which is fine by me."

"How's your schoolin'?"

"Fine."

There's silence and not much to talk about between Olivia and Maggie. The two have never been close. Olivia always saw Maggie as a strange, cold-hearted person. Crystal starts squirming.

Maggie, getting a little agitated, complains, "It's acting weird."

"It's a girl, Maggie."

"Well…I don't like it. You take it."

"Just hang on a sec…I gotta finish this stitch. Just rock her a bit…"

"Rock her?"

"Ya know…rocka bye baby on the tree top…just gently rock her…"

Maggie looks at Crystal, squirming, and starts rocking her slowly, and then seeing that Crystal reacts to it, starts getting a little more aggressive. Maggie's eyes change as she watches the reaction on Crystal's face. Olivia is engrossed in her sewing and does not see at first. Then, as Maggie's rocking approaches a full swing, Crystal lets out a cry. Olivia looks up terrified…Maggie is entranced. "Maggie! What the hell are you doing? Stop right now!"

Crystal is fully crying. Maggie looks at Olivia and then stops. "Okay."

Olivia quickly drops everything and goes over, and takes Crystal, consoling her with powerful love. Crystal begins to relax. "What the hell did you think you were doing?"

Maggie looks at Olivia with the flat emotion of Eddie. The penny drops for Olivia…and then a hint of smoke… "I…I'm sorry…I wasn't trying to hurt her on purpose…"

Maggie keeps looking at Olivia and Crystal as Olivia turns her attention to the front door where she hears footsteps. Frank walks in, staggering. "Hey Frank," Olivia says.

Frank looks at Olivia, and then Maggie, and then back to Olivia. "Get upstairs."

"Frank…Maggie's here…can't you…"

Frank flies at Olivia, hits her hard across the face and grabs her arm. "Get upstairs now!"

Maggie stands up in a fury, she is young, but her eyes have clicked. "You let her go!"

Frank hit Maggie. "You stay out of this."

Olivia turns to Maggie "Maggie…you just go home…it's okay. We can talk tomorrow."

Olivia looks at Maggie, and Maggie backs down, looking at Frank. Olivia then drops her eyes to the table. "Okay…"

She walks past to put Crystal in the crib that sits in the living room. Frank goes and waits at the bottom of the stairs for Olivia.

Olivia gently puts Crystal down with a kiss and then goes to Frank. He puts his hand on her face and then on her breast. "Good."

He then turns to Maggie who is still standing at the table, as he molests Olivia. "You make sure that door is closed when you leave, little girl."

Maggie says nothing, but remains still until she hears Olivia and Frank walking up the stairs and then walks out the front door.

Later that night, when Frank was done having his way with Olivia, he went out drinking. He was drinking a lot, even in his car. Suddenly, when he reached down to grab another bottle, he lost control of the car and was killed immediately upon impact.

When Olivia found out the news from the police who had come to her house, she took it fairly hard. After all, Frank was the father of her children.

***

By this time, Olivia, Jennifer, and Dexter are back inside sitting down at the dining room table. Jennifer wanting to know more, asks, "Olivia…Are you and Maggie…still talking? …"

Olivia shakes her head. "Oh no…Maggie lives on the other side of town, but we don't see each other…we never really saw each other. I didn't want to see her or talk to her…What I saw that day in her eyes… well see…I can't have that in my life or in my children's life. I know now to just go to the smoke…to go to where GOD points me…see, I never really knew what all that smoke was. Those little wisps that I would see before God was about to intervene, I was working again and trying to just figure it all out…"

***

Olivia is in the nurse's office at the hospital working the graveyard shift. She sits at her desk with the door open to the main hall. The halls are dark and quiet with the exception of the occasional beep of a machine and the hum of florescent lights. Olivia is writing down notes in a large block slanted script. They are dollar amounts…rent… salary…groceries…she is trying to figure out how to make ends meet with Frank no longer here.

Olivia had always kept money aside that Frank didn't know about. Tiny always told her to keep some money away "cause men didn't know what to do with it. They just spend it on themselves and all". Although she had some money, she didn't see how she and the kids were going to make it without Frank's money. Ironically, money made Olivia more scared than she had ever been with Frank, so she started praying right at her desk.

Olivia puts the pencil down. Her eyes are wet with the beginnings of tears, and she looks worried and scared. She looks at a picture of Frank Jr. and Crystal that she has on her desk. Then, she crosses herself, closes her eyes and begins a silent prayer.

Olivia takes in a deep breath, and then another. Then she opens her eyes, and the room is filled with the same translucent, lacey smoke, but now thicker and more substantial. She does not smell it, but feels it…and it pulls her up. She moves out into the corridor and the hall is filled with smoke. It's thick, but Olivia can see everything. She walks, following the richness of the smoke.

It takes her to a hospital room at the end of the hall. The name on the door is Olivia Clark. Olivia pauses but moves in. There is someone laying in the hospital bed. Olivia approaches it. It appears the smoke is emanating through the blankets to cover the hospital floor. As Olivia looks at the body, she sees it is hers. Yet, it is abused, beaten, every injury she suffered from Eddie or Frank is seen on her skin…and she is dying. Olivia walks up to herself, sits down next to her and takes her hand. She holds her hand tight as her dying self looks at her, and smiles.

Suddenly, Olivia Clark transforms into a rush of smoke that pulls upwards through the ceiling and into dark space. Olivia follows the smoke that transforms into a bright corona of radiant light.

Dawn is breaking and there is another nurse walking down the hall looking for someone. She enters the nurses' office. "Olivia?"

Seeing that Olivia is not there, the nurse leaves and walks down the hall, peaking in patients' rooms. Another nurse walks by and she stops her. "Have you seen Olivia?"

The nurse shakes her head. "No…I haven't seen her all morning…"

The nurse that is looking for Olivia continues walking down the hall and finds the room where Olivia met Olivia Clark, but the name tag by the door is blank. She looks in and sees someone laying on what should be an empty patient bed. "Olivia?"

The sleeping body turns. It is Olivia and she looks back at the nurse. "Yeah…I'm sorry…I…"

The nurse, initially angry, looks at Olivia who has clearly been crying. Her face is soaked with tears, but her countenance is happy and elated. The nurse walks in and sits in the chair next to her. "Are you okay?"

"I'm better than I have ever been."

The nurse confused, says, "Okay…but let's maybe not let it happen again, okay? Or at least, not while at work."

"Of course." Olivia gets up with enormous strength and courage, and walks out of the hospital room.

***

Jennifer, Dexter, and Olivia are still sitting together, but now, the sun is slowly starting to set. Jennifer, wanting to know more, asks, "You never married again?"

"No. That was 1962. I knew I was stronger on my own."

"But you had three kids…"

"Carolyn was born in 1968…about 6 years later…but me and her father never married. We didn't have no problems…and I never depended on him. I just didn't want to get married again.

Maybe that seems off or…like I wasn't being true maybe…but see, in all this, what I learned was that in me is the strength of a lion. I can take whatever the world throws at me…whatever the challenges are because if I love…If I love my GOD, and If I love my beautiful children…and now my grandchildren…If I love, well, then I have the strength of a lion. And that strength is 10 times more than what any man can give me. And it sure as hell is stronger than any evil that anyone can throw my way."

Olivia closes her eyes and prays in silence.

Jennifer hesitates…thinking…then reaches for Olivia's hand and holds it. Jennifer closes her eyes as Olivia says these words, a shared prayer between the two. As Olivia finishes, they open their eyes and look at each other with a shared strength in their sisterhood, understood for the first time since their meeting. They break their stare.

Dexter, trying not to be rude but wanting to know more, asks, "Olivia…what happened to Diane? …"

"I don't know if you want to know Dexter…maybe we should just leave it there…"

"Well…did she find God too?"

"No…Diane tried…she tried to find GOD. She worked at a Church for years…even lived there. She learned to cook and had a good job…and she tried. She needed the discipline of a good home, the peace and safety of a church. She was very spiritual. Her faith was in GOD. I just wish she could have been happy with only GOD's love. But despite all she'd been through, and her faith, she still needed a man in her life…I wish she could have just stayed in the church… but…years later, she left and got her a job driving a school bus for handicapped children in this city."

***

The year is 1975, and Diane, who is 41, is driving a handicapped school bus that pulls up to a neighborhood home. She parks and goes in back of the bus to find Romeo, a ten year old boy with a severe physical and mental handicap. A neck rest holds his head in place, but when he sees Diane, he manages a smile, and Diane smiles back. "Hey Romeo! We're home. You ready to go see mom and dad?"

Diane genuinely and warmly touches Romeo, and gently removes his wheelchair from the brackets. She then maneuvers him out of the bus up to the family home, pushing his chair up a ramp. Romeo's mom comes out to greet Romeo and Diane, who warmly passes on the responsibility for Romeo's care.

Diane loves taking care of kids, but she isn't happy.

Diane walks back to the bus, the genuine smile she just had now gone as she boards the bus and drives away.

Later that night, Diane tries to find her happiness by going out to a night club. She is looking for a man to make her whole. She meets Skippy, a white salesman, at the bar. They flirt, talk, and dance all night. They leave the bar laughing and go out to his car. There is a rack with shirts in the back seat. They push them aside and fall to the ground as they have sex in the back seat.

Skippy lives in a small city but has money, and seems like a good man. He comes in during the week for sales, and stays with Diane, buying her things and treating her special. It seems as though he genuinely loves her. A few years later in 1978, they get married and he moves in with Diane, but still travels as a salesman.

16

At Diane's apartment, she, Olivia, a few girlfriends, and Isadore, her best friend, are sitting around a table with wine and beer bottles, laughing and talking. After being caught up in laughter, Diane starts coughing. The table stops as the coughing seems more than just something simple…she stops. "Sorry…just a little cough I'm fighting is all…what were we all talking about? …"

Isadore concerned, asks, "You sure Diane?"

"I'm fine…pass me the wine would you? A little wine never hurts…"

Isadore smirks, "You got that right, girl."

Isadore pours a large glass for Diane, and the two clink glasses before taking a nice swig as Olivia looks on. She thinks back to what her Momma said about always having girlfriends over your house. She said it was like, "starting a fire when you have your girlfriends around your man."

Skippy walks into the front door of the apartment, and Diane gets up quickly to greet him. She gives him a warm hug and kiss, and then breaks away with a cough. Skippy reaches over to her. "You okay there, sweetie pie? Not getting any better?"

Diane trying to smile, says, "No…it's fine…just lingering around is all. Come, let's get you a drink."

Skippy and Diane walk into the dining room. "Hello ladies… my…what a fine sight to come home to…"

Skippy sits in Diane's chair as Diane goes to the kitchen to get him a beer. Skippy looks at Isadore and they share a loving smile.

Skippy, not taking his eyes off Isadore, asks, "And how have all of you been?"

Olivia, looking at Skippy, responds, "We've been fine…"

Skippy gives no response. He is too busy dazing off at Isadore. Olivia repeats herself. "Skippy…I said we've been fine…and how 'bout you?"

Skippy finally looks at Olivia. "Well you know, Olivia…been missing my lovely Diane…Diane? You okay? You get my beer there?"

Diane walks out of the kitchen, there is some blood on her blouse. She brings the beer to Skippy. "Sorry Skippy…just had a little accident…I'll be right back…"

Diane sets the beer on the counter, but it has a cap on it. Diane runs off.

Skippy showing no empathy, whines, "What am I supposed to do with a bottle that's got a cap…"

Isadore jumps up, "Oh…I'll go get you the opener."

Isadore gets up and goes into the kitchen. "Skippy…where is the bottle opener?"

"It's in the…oh here…"

Skippy gets up to go help Isadore in the kitchen. Olivia sits at the table and waits…then gets concerned about Diane and goes to find her in the bathroom. She knocks at the door. "Diane? You okay?"

"Yeah Olivia…I'm fine, but I got this stain on my shirt. Can you go grab some cleaner from under the kitchen sink so I can scrub this out now?"

"Yeah."

Olivia walks across the apartment to the kitchen. As she walks in, she finds Skippy and Isadore kissing by the sink. "What…?"

Isadore pulls away from Skippy. "Oh…it's…I'll be…"

Isadore just walks out, and Skippy smiles after her. Olivia looks at Skippy with a cold, hard stare. He looks back...colder. Olivia looks down and goes to get the cleaner, forcing Skippy to move.

Skippy tries to lighten the atmosphere. "Don't you trouble yourself over that now Olivia...that ain't nothing."

Olivia gets the cleaner out from the sink. "I am gonna trouble myself with it, Skippy...and you should be troubling yourself with Diane. You are a married man, and you have a sick wife. You know she looking worse every time I see her. She had that cough now for over a month, and what are you doing about it?"

Skippy steps closer. "Look Olivia...don't you trouble yourself at all...she ain't gonna live that long anyhow."

"What?!?"

Skippy walks out of the kitchen. "I said don't you trouble yourself."

Olivia stands in the kitchen, not believing what she just heard. A cold chill goes all through her body.

Skippy, in the other room, says, "Alright ladies...looks like I'm gonna have to take care of my beautiful wife now...so let's everyone get up and go."

Skippy pauses and then looks back at Olivia. "Come on now Olivia...you bring me that cleaner and get going, so Diane can get her rest..."

Olivia walks slowly out of the kitchen and sees as Isadore and the other girls are all walking out the door.

Skippy still looking at Olivia, says, "Come on...get going now. Don't you trouble."

Olivia walks out, and the door closes behind her. She stands, turns to the door and turns back...scared. She closes her eyes and prays. She thought to mention to her sister when she talked to her later that she caught Skippy and Isadore kissing in the kitchen. Then, she remembered when she brought up her suspicions to Diane last time; she told Olivia she was messing up her day. So, she left it alone, and continues to pray for her sister.

A few days later, Diane was found stabbed to death in the apartment. Someone had broken in and stole a lot of expensive jewelry. When Olivia found out the news about her sister, her heart was torn wide open.

***

The sun has set, but Olivia is still continuing with her story. "We all knew who it was. Never could prove a thing and the police, well, they just figured it was your typical black on black crime. For Diane to have lived her whole life in such a horrific way and then to die in such a violent way, I know God had his arms wrapped around her."

Jennifer, upset, asks, "Did you at least talk to the police?"

"I tried…but no one ever listened. See, being a black woman in that time…it was hard to have a voice Jennifer…so hard."

"Things are better now?"

"Better…but still the same. But we must keep fighting…alone and together. With our family…with GOD…we must keep fighting."

Olivia gets up. "Now…I think you two best get going…I need to rest up a bit now…my back is screaming."

Jennifer looks at Olivia. "You've changed me, Olivia."

Olivia looks hard at Jennifer. "No…You change yourself…don't let someone change you. You be strong. You only change if you want to…you got that?"

"Yeah."

Olivia motions for Jennifer to stand up. She does and Olivia gives her a hug.

Jennifer starts to get a little emotional. "Thank you, Olivia."

"Anytime…now come back. Let's keep each other strong, okay?"

Jennifer smiles. "You bet."

"You too Dexter…don't you just call me when you have some pretty girl to show off now…"

Dexter blushes. "You bet Olivia."

Dexter and Jennifer both walk out the front door and down the front walkway to Jennifer's truck, and drive off. Soon enough, Jennifer's truck is parked in the driveway and the two of them are sitting there staring at Dexter's house.

Jennifer is still thinking about Olivia's life. "I can't imagine having her life. I just can't...and being strong and happy as she is...and loving...it's just..."

Jennifer reaches for the cross around her neck. It reminds her that that is how it makes sense...she nods. Dexter does not see her. "I know. I don't get it. I am all angry and shit just thinking about everything...you'd think after her life, you must want to just yell and scream and...well...I don't know."

"She's amazing."

Dexter agrees, "You got that right."

They both pause in silence. Dexter then looks at Jennifer. "You alright? You wanna come in? If I'm smelling right, there's a barbecue going on around here somewhere."

"No Dexter...I'm gonna go home before it gets dark."

"Suit yourself."

Jennifer looks at Dexter intensely. "Thanks Dexter...for everything...for introducing me to Olivia...she's life-changing."

"No problem...but don't you be changing unless you want to, girl."

They both smile. "You bet."

Dexter gets out of the car and walks up to the house. A guy and girl sitting on the porch of the next house say something to Dexter. He walks over to their house as the man gets up and goes off the porch to greet Dexter. They shake hands, hug, and start talking like old friends. Jennifer watches. She stares at them, looks at her car, her hands, and closes her eyes and prays. She turns off the car and gets out. "Hey Dex...I think, yeah...I'd like to hang out...that cool?"

"Hell yeah, girl...come on over here...let me introduce you."

Jennifer joins Dexter and his neighbors. They all shake hands and go back to their porch, and just laugh and talk about life. Then Jennifer thinks to herself about Olivia and the strength they share from sisterhood. She knows to always keep her promise…she'll never change unless she wants to…

Printed in the United States
By Bookmasters